Beowulf

An Anglo-Saxon Epic Poem

Translated by

JNO: Lesslie Hall, Ph.D. (J.H.U.)

Professor of English and History in the College of
William and Mary

To my Wife

NATAL PUBLISHING LLC
ARS LONGA, VITA BREVIS

Contents

Preface

THE present work is a modest effort to reproduce approximately, in modern measures, the venerable epic, Beowulf. *Approximately*, I repeat; for a very close reproduction of Anglo-Saxon verse would, to a large extent, be prose to a modern ear.

The Heyne-Socin text and glossary have been closely followed. Occasionally a deviation has been made, but always for what seemed good and sufficient reason. The translator does not aim to be an editor. Once in a while, however, he has added a conjecture of his own to the emendations quoted from the criticisms of other students of the poem.

This work is addressed to two classes of readers. From both of these alike the translator begs sympathy and co-operation. The Anglo-Saxon scholar he hopes to please by adhering faithfully to the original. The student of English literature he aims to interest by giving him, in modern garb, the most ancient epic of our race. This is a bold and venturesome undertaking; and yet there must be some students of the Teutonic past willing to follow even a daring guide, if they may read in modern phrases of the sorrows of Hrothgar, of the prowess of Beowulf, and of the feelings that stirred the hearts of our forefathers in their primeval homes.

In order to please the larger class of readers, a regular cadence has been used, a measure which, while retaining the essential characteristics of the original, permits the reader to see ahead of him in reading.

Perhaps every Anglo-Saxon scholar has his own theory as to how Beowulf should be translated. Some have given us prose versions of what we believe to be a great poem. Is it any reflection on our honored Kemble and Arnold to say that their translations fail to show a layman that Beowulf is justly called our first *epic*? Of those translators who have used verse, several have written [viii]from what would seem a mistaken point of view. Is it proper, for instance, that the grave and solemn speeches of Beowulf and Hrothgar be put in ballad measures, tripping lightly and airily along? Or, again, is it fitting that the rough martial music of Anglo-Saxon verse be interpreted to us in the smooth measures of modern blank verse? Do we hear what has been beautifully called "the clanging tread of a warrior in mail"?

Of all English translations of Beowulf, that of Professor Garnett alone gives any adequate idea of the chief characteristics of this great Teutonic epic.

The measure used in the present translation is believed to be as near a reproduction of the original as modern English affords. The cadences closely resemble those used by Browning in some of his most striking poems. The four stresses of the Anglo-Saxon verse are retained, and as much thesis and anacrusis is allowed as is consistent with a regular cadence. Alliteration has been used to a large extent; but it was thought that modern ears would hardly tolerate it on every line. End-rhyme has been used occasionally; internal rhyme, sporadically. Both have some warrant in Anglo-Saxon poetry. (For end-rhyme, see 1 53, 1 54; for internal rhyme, 2 21, 6 40.)

What Gummere[1] calls the "rime-giver" has been studiously kept; *viz.*, the first accented syllable in the second half-verse always carries the alliteration; and the last accented syllable alliterates only sporadically. Alternate alliteration is occasionally used as in the original. (See 7 61, 8 5.)

No two accented syllables have been brought together, except occasionally after a cæsural pause. (See 2 19 and 12 1.) Or, scientifically speaking, Sievers's C type has been avoided as not consonant with the plan of translation. Several of his types, however, constantly occur; *e.g.* A and a variant (/ x | / x) (/ x x | / x); B and a variant (x / | x /) (x x / | x /); a variant of D (/ x | / x x); E (/ x x | /). Anacrusis gives further variety to the types used in the translation.

The parallelisms of the original have been faithfully preserved. (*E.g.*, 1 16 and 1 17: "Lord" and "Wielder of Glory"; 1 30, 1 31, 1 32; 2 12 and 2 13; 2 27 and 2 28; 3 5 and 3 6.) Occasionally, some loss has been sustained; but, on the other hand, a gain has here and there been made.

The effort has been made to give a decided flavor of archaism to the translation. All words not in keeping with the spirit of the poem have been [ix]avoided. Again, though many archaic words have been used, there are none, it is believed, which are not found in standard modern poetry.

With these preliminary remarks, it will not be amiss to give an outline of the story of the poem.

---

[1] Handbook of Poetics, page 175, 1st edition.

The Story

Hrothgar, king of the Danes, or Scyldings, builds a great mead-hall, or palace, in which he hopes to feast his liegemen and to give them presents. The joy of king and retainers is, however, of short duration. Grendel, the monster, is seized with hateful jealousy. He cannot brook the sounds of joyance that reach him down in his fen-dwelling near the hall. Oft and anon he goes to the joyous building, bent on direful mischief. Thane after thane is ruthlessly carried off and devoured, while no one is found strong enough and bold enough to cope with the monster. For twelve years he persecutes Hrothgar and his vassals.

Over sea, a day's voyage off, Beowulf, of the Geats, nephew of Higelac, king of the Geats, hears of Grendel's doings and of Hrothgar's misery. He resolves to crush the fell monster and relieve the aged king. With fourteen chosen companions, he sets sail for Dane-land. Reaching that country, he soon persuades Hrothgar of his ability to help him. The hours that elapse before night are spent in beer-drinking and conversation. When Hrothgar's bedtime comes he leaves the hall in charge of Beowulf, telling him that never before has he given to another the absolute wardship of his palace. All retire to rest, Beowulf, as it were, sleeping upon his arms.

Grendel comes, the great march-stepper, bearing God's anger. He seizes and kills one of the sleeping warriors. Then he advances towards Beowulf. A fierce and desperate hand-to-hand struggle ensues. No arms are used, both combatants trusting to strength and hand-grip. Beowulf tears Grendel's shoulder from its socket, and the monster retreats to his den, howling and yelling with agony and fury. The wound is fatal.

The next morning, at early dawn, warriors in numbers flock to the hall Heorot, to hear the news. Joy is boundless. Glee runs high. Hrothgar and his retainers are lavish of gratitude and of gifts.

Grendel's mother, however, comes the next night to avenge his death. She is furious and raging. While Beowulf is sleeping in a room somewhat apart [x]from the quarters of the other warriors, she seizes one of Hrothgar's favorite counsellors, and carries him off and devours him. Beowulf is called. Determined to leave Heorot entirely purified, he arms himself, and goes down to look for the female monster. After traveling through the waters many hours, he meets her near the sea-bottom. She drags him to her den. There he sees Grendel lying dead. After a desperate and almost fatal struggle with the woman, he slays her, and swims upward in triumph, taking with him Grendel's head.

Joy is renewed at Heorot. Congratulations crowd upon the

victor. Hrothgar literally pours treasures into the lap of Beowulf; and it is agreed among the vassals of the king that Beowulf will be their next liegelord.

Beowulf leaves Dane-land. Hrothgar weeps and laments at his departure.

When the hero arrives in his own land, Higelac treats him as a distinguished guest. He is the hero of the hour.

Beowulf subsequently becomes king of his own people, the Geats. After he has been ruling for fifty years, his own neighborhood is wofully harried by a fire-spewing dragon. Beowulf determines to kill him. In the ensuing struggle both Beowulf and the dragon are slain. The grief of the Geats is inexpressible. They determine, however, to leave nothing undone to honor the memory of their lord. A great funeral-pyre is built, and his body is burnt. Then a memorial-barrow is made, visible from a great distance, that sailors afar may be constantly reminded of the prowess of the national hero of Geatland.

The poem closes with a glowing tribute to his bravery, his gentleness, his goodness of heart, and his generosity.

It is the devout desire of this translator to hasten the day when the story of Beowulf shall be as familiar to English-speaking peoples as that of the Iliad. Beowulf is our first great epic. It is an epitomized history of the life of the Teutonic races. It brings vividly before us our forefathers of pre-Alfredian eras, in their love of war, of sea, and of adventure.

My special thanks are due to Professors Francis A. March and James A. Harrison, for advice, sympathy, and assistance.

J.L. HALL.

Abbreviations Used in the Notes

B = Bugge.

C. = Cosijn.

Gr. = Grein.

Grdvtg. = Grundtvig.

H. = Heyne.

H. and S. = Harrison and Sharp.

H.-So. = Heyne-Socin.

K.= Kemble.

Kl. = Kluge.

M.= Müllenhoff.

R. = Rieger.

S. = Sievers.

Sw. = Sweet.

t.B. = ten Brink.

Th. = Thorpe.

W. = Wülcker

Bibliography of Translations

Arnold, Thomas.—Beowulf. A heroic poem of the eighth century. London, 1876. With English translation. Prose.

Botkine, L.—Beowulf. Epopée Anglo-Saxonne. Havre, 1877. First French translation. Passages occasionally omitted.

Conybeare, J.J.—Illustrations of Anglo-Saxon Poetry. London, 1826. Full Latin translation, and some passages translated into English blank-verse.

Ettmuller, L.—Beowulf, stabreimend übersetzt. Zürich, 1840.

Garnett, J.M.—Beowulf: an Anglo-Saxon Poem, and the Fight at Finnsburg. Boston, 1882. An accurate line-for-line translation, using alliteration occasionally, and sometimes assuming a metrical cadence.

Grein, C.W.M.—Dichtungen der Angelsachsen, stabreimend übersetzt. 2 Bde. Göttingen, 1857-59.

Grion, Giusto.—Beovulf, poema epico anglo-sassone del VII. secolo, tradotto e illustrato. Lucca, 1883. First Italian translation.

Grundtvig, N.F.S.—Bjowulfs Drape. Copenhagen, 1820.

Heyne, M.—A translation in iambic measures. Paderborn, 1863.

Kemble, J.M.—The Anglo-Saxon Poems of Beowulf, the Traveller's Song, and the Battle of Finnsburg. London, 1833. The second edition contains a prose translation of Beowulf.

Leo, H.—Ueber Beowulf. Halle, 1839. Translations of extracts.

Lumsden, H.W.—Beowulf, translated into modern rhymes. London, 1881. Ballad measures. Passages occasionally omitted.

Sandras, G.S.—De carminibus Cædmoni adjudicatis. Paris, 1859. An extract from Beowulf, with Latin translation.

Schaldmose, F.—Beowulf og Scopes Widsith, to Angelsaxiske Digte. Copenhagen, 1847.

Simrock, K.—Beowulf. Uebersetzt und erläutert. Stuttgart und Augsburg, 1859. Alliterative measures.

Thorkelin, G.J.—De Danorum rebus gestis secul. III. et IV. poema Danicum dialecto Anglosaxonica. Havniæ, 1815. Latin translation.

Thorpe, B.—The Anglo-Saxon Poems of Beowulf, the Scôp or Gleeman's Tale, and the Fight at Finnsburg. Oxford, 1855. English translation in short lines, generally containing two stresses.

Wackerbarth, A.D.—Beowulf, translated into English verse. London, 1849.

Wickberg, R.—Beowulf, en fornengelsk hjeltedikt, öfersatt. Westervik. First Swedish translation.

von Wolzogen, H.—Beowulf, in alliterative measures. Leipzig.

Zinsser, G.—Der Kampf Beowulfs mit Grendel. Jahresbericht of the Realschule at Forbach, 1881.

Glossary of Proper Names

[The figures refer to the divisions of the poem in which the respective names occur. The initial figures refer to fitts, the secondary, to lines in the fitts.]

Ælfhere.—A kinsman of Wiglaf.—36 3.

Æschere.—Confidential friend of King Hrothgar. Elder brother of Yrmenlaf. Killed by Grendel.—21 3; 30 89.

Beanstan.—Father of Breca.—9 26.

Beowulf.—Son of Scyld, the founder of the dynasty of Scyldings. Father of Healfdene, and grandfather of Hrothgar.— 1 18; 2 1.

Beowulf.—The hero of the poem. Sprung from the stock of Geats, son of Ecgtheow. Brought up by his maternal grandfather Hrethel, and figuring in manhood as a devoted liegeman of his uncle Higelac. A hero from his youth. Has the strength of thirty men. Engages in a swimming-match with Breca. Goes to the help of Hrothgar against the monster Grendel. Vanquishes Grendel and his mother. Afterwards becomes king of the Geats. Late in life attempts to kill a fire-spewing dragon, and is slain. Is buried with great honors. His memorial mound.— 6 26; 7 2; 7 9; 9 3; 9 8; 12 28; 12 43; 23 1, etc.

Breca.—Beowulf's opponent in the famous swimming-match.— 9 8; 9 19; 9 21; 9 22.

Brondings.—A people ruled by Breca.—9 23.

Brosinga mene.—A famous collar once owned by the Brosings.— 19 7.

Cain.—Progenitor of Grendel and other monsters.—2 56; 20 11.

Dæghrefn.—A warrior of the Hugs, killed by Beowulf.—35 40.

Danes.—Subjects of Scyld and his descendants, and hence often called Scyldings. Other names for them are Victory-Scyldings, Honor-Scyldings, Armor-Danes, Bright-Danes, East-Danes, West-Danes, North-Danes, South-Danes, Ingwins, Hrethmen.—1 1; 2 1; 3 2; 5 14; 7 1, etc.

Ecglaf.—Father of Unferth, who taunts Beowulf.—9 1.

Ecgtheow.—Father of Beowulf, the hero of the poem. A widely-known Wægmunding warrior. Marries Hrethel's daughter. After slaying Heatholaf, a Wylfing, he flees his country.—7 3; 5 6; 8 4.

Ecgwela.—A king of the Danes before Scyld.—25 60.

[xiv]

Elan.—Sister of Hrothgar, and probably wife of Ongentheow, king of the Swedes.—2 10.

Eagle Cape.—A promontory in Geat-land, under which took place Beowulf's last encounter.—41 87.

Eadgils.—Son of Ohthere and brother of Eanmund.—34 2.

Eanmund.—Son of Ohthere and brother of Eadgils. The reference to these brothers is vague, and variously understood. Heyne supposes as follows: Raising a revolt against their father, they are obliged to leave Sweden. They go to the land of the Geats; with what intention, is not known, but probably to conquer and plunder. The Geatish king, Heardred, is slain by one of the brothers, probably Eanmund.—36 10; 31 54 to 31 60; 33 66 to 34 6.

Eofor.—A Geatish hero who slays Ongentheow in war, and is rewarded by Hygelac with the hand of his only daughter.—41 18; 41 48.

Eormenric.—A Gothic king, from whom Hama took away the famous Brosinga mene.—19 9.

Eomær.—Son of Offa and Thrytho, king and queen of the Angles.—28 69.

Finn.—King of the North-Frisians and the Jutes. Marries Hildeburg. At his court takes place the horrible slaughter in which the Danish general, Hnæf, fell. Later on, Finn himself is slain by Danish warriors.— 17 18; 17 30; 17 44; 18 4; 18 23.

Fin-land.—The country to which Beowulf was driven by the currents in his swimming-match.—10 22.

Fitela.—Son and nephew of King Sigemund, whose praises are sung in XIV.—14 42; 14 53.

Folcwalda.—Father of Finn.—17 38.

Franks.—Introduced occasionally in referring to the death of Higelac.—19 19; 40 21; 40 24.

Frisians.—A part of them are ruled by Finn. Some of them were engaged in the struggle in which Higelac was slain.— 17 20; 17 42; 17 52; 40 21.

Freaware.—Daughter of King Hrothgar. Married to Ingeld, a Heathobard prince.—29 60; 30 32.

Froda.—King of the Heathobards, and father of Ingeld.—29 62.

Garmund.—Father of Offa.—28 71.

Geats, Geatmen.—The race to which the hero of the poem belongs. Also called Weder-Geats, or Weders, War-Geats, Sea-Geats. They are ruled by Hrethel, Hæthcyn, Higelac, and Beowulf.—4 7; 7 4; 10 45; 11 8; 27 14; 28 8.

Gepids.—Named in connection with the Danes and Swedes.— 35 34.

Grendel.—A monster of the race of Cain. Dwells in the fens and moors. Is furiously envious when he hears sounds of joy in Hrothgar's palace. Causes the king untold agony for years. Is finally conquered by Beowulf, and dies of his wound. His hand and arm are hung up in Hrothgar's hall Heorot. His head is cut off by Beowulf when he goes down to fight with Grendel's mother.—2 50; 3 1; 3 13; 8 19; 11 17; 12 2; 13 27; 15 3.

Guthlaf.—A Dane of Hnæf's party.—18 24.

Half-Danes.—Branch of the Danes to which Hnæf belonged.—17 19.

Halga.—Surnamed the Good. Younger brother of Hrothgar.—2 9.

Hama.—Takes the Brosinga mene from Eormenric.—19 7.

Hæreth.—Father of Higelac's queen, Hygd.—28 39; 29 18.

Hæthcyn.—Son of Hrethel and brother of Higelac. Kills his brother Herebeald accidentally. Is slain at Ravenswood, fighting against Ongentheow.—34 43; 35 23; 40 32.

Helmings.—The race to which Queen Wealhtheow belonged.—10 63.

Heming.—A kinsman of Garmund, perhaps nephew.—28 54; 28 70.

Hengest.—A Danish leader. Takes command on the fall of Hnæf.—17 33; 17 41.

Herebeald.—Eldest son of Hrethel, the Geatish king, and brother of Higelac. Killed by his younger brother Hæthcyn.—34 43; 34 47.

Heremod.—A Danish king of a dynasty before the Scylding line. Was a source of great sorrow to his people.—14 64; 25 59.

Hereric.—Referred to as uncle of Heardred, but otherwise unknown.—31 60.

Hetwars.—Another name for the Franks.—33 51.

Healfdene.—Grandson of Scyld and father of Hrothgar. Ruled the Danes long and well.—2 5; 4 1; 8 14.

Heardred.—Son of Higelac and Hygd, king and queen of the Geats. Succeeds his father, with Beowulf as regent. Is slain by the sons of Ohthere.—31 56; 33 63; 33 75.

Heathobards.—Race of Lombards, of which Froda is king. After Froda falls in battle with the Danes, Ingeld, his son, marries Hrothgar's daughter, Freaware, in order to heal the feud.—30 1; 30 6.

Heatholaf.—A Wylfing warrior slain by Beowulf's father.—8 5.

Heathoremes.—The people on whose shores Breca is cast by the waves during his contest with Beowulf.—9 21.

Heorogar.—Elder brother of Hrothgar, and surnamed 'Weoroda Ræswa,' Prince of the Troopers.—2 9; 8 12.

Hereward.—Son of the above.—31 17.

Heort, Heorot.—The great mead-hall which King Hrothgar builds. It is invaded by Grendel for twelve years. Finally cleansed by Beowulf, the Geat. It is called Heort on account of the hart-antlers which decorate it.—2 25; 3 32; 3 52.

Hildeburg.—Wife of Finn, daughter of Hoce, and related to Hnæf,—probably his sister.—17 21; 18 34.

Hnæf.—Leader of a branch of the Danes called Half-Danes. Killed in the struggle at Finn's castle.—17 19; 17 61.

Hondscio.—One of Beowulf's companions. Killed by Grendel just before Beowulf grappled with that monster.—30 43.

Hoce.—Father of Hildeburg and probably of Hnæf.—17 26.

Hrethel.—King of the Geats, father of Higelac, and grandfather of Beowulf.—7 4; 34 39.

Hrethla.—Once used for Hrethel.—7 82.

Hrethmen.—Another name for the Danes.—7 73.

Hrethric.—Son of Hrothgar.—18 65; 27 19.

Hreosna-beorh.—A promontory in Geat-land, near which Ohthere's sons made plundering raids.—35 18.

Hrothgar.—The Danish king who built the hall Heort, but was long unable to enjoy it on account of Grendel's persecutions. Marries Wealhtheow, a Helming lady. Has two sons and a daughter. Is a typical Teutonic king, lavish of gifts. A devoted liegelord, as his lamentations over slain liegemen prove. Also very appreciative of kindness, as is shown by his loving gratitude to Beowulf.— 2 9; 2 12; 4 1; 8 10; 15 1; etc., etc.

Hrothmund.—Son of Hrothgar.—18 65.

Hrothulf.—Probably a son of Halga, younger brother of Hrothgar. Certainly on terms of close intimacy in Hrothgar's palace.—16 26; 18 57.

Hrunting.—Unferth's sword, lent to Beowulf.—22 71; 25 9.

Hugs.—A race in alliance with the Franks and Frisians at the time of Higelac's fall.—35 41.

Hun.—A Frisian warrior, probably general of the Hetwars. Gives Hengest a beautiful sword.—18 19.

Hunferth.—Sometimes used for Unferth.

Hygelac, Higelac.—King of the Geats, uncle and liegelord of Beowulf, the hero of the poem.—His second wife is the lovely Hygd, daughter of Hæreth. The son of their union is Heardred. Is slain in a war with the Hugs, Franks, and Frisians combined. Beowulf is regent, and afterwards king of the Geats.—4 6; 5 4; 28 34; 29 9; 29 21; 31 56.

Hygd.—Wife of Higelac, and daughter of Hæreth. There are some indications that she married Beowulf after she became a

goes to look for Grendel's mother. In the MS. sometimes written *Hunferth*. 9 1; 18 41.

Wæls.—Father of Sigemund.—14 60.

Wægmunding.—A name occasionally applied to Wiglaf and Beowulf, and perhaps derived from a common ancestor, Wægmund.—36 6; 38 61.

Weders.—Another name for Geats or Wedergeats.

Wayland.—A fabulous smith mentioned in this poem and in other old Teutonic literature.—7 83.

Wendels.—The people of Wulfgar, Hrothgar's messenger and retainer. (Perhaps = Vandals.)—6 30.

Wealhtheow.—Wife of Hrothgar. Her queenly courtesy is well shown in the poem.—10 55.

Weohstan, or **Wihstan**.—A Wægmunding, and father of Wiglaf.—36 1.

Whale's Ness.—A prominent promontory, on which Beowulf's mound was built.—38 52; 42 76.

Wiglaf.—Son of Wihstan, and related to Beowulf. He remains faithful to Beowulf in the fatal struggle with the fire-drake. Would rather die than leave his lord in his dire emergency.—36 1; 36 3; 36 28.

Wonred.—Father of Wulf and Eofor.—41 20; 41 26.

Wulf.—Son of Wonred. Engaged in the battle between Higelac's and Ongentheow's forces, and had a hand-to-hand fight with Ongentheow himself. Ongentheow disables him, and is thereupon slain by Eofor.—41 19; 41 29.

Wulfgar.—Lord of the Wendels, and retainer of Hrothgar.—6 18; 6 30.

Wylfings.—A people to whom belonged Heatholaf, who was slain by Ecgtheow.—8 6; 8 16.

Yrmenlaf.—Younger brother of Æschere, the hero whose death grieved Hrothgar so deeply.—21 4.

List of Words and Phrases Not in General Use

ATHELING.—Prince, nobleman.
BAIRN.—Son, child.
BARROW.—Mound, rounded hill, funeral-mound.
BATTLE-SARK.—Armor.
BEAKER.—Cup, drinking-vessel.
BEGEAR.—Prepare.
BIGHT.—Bay, sea.
BILL.—Sword.
BOSS.—Ornamental projection.
BRACTEATE.—A round ornament on a necklace.
BRAND.—Sword.
BURN.—Stream.
BURNIE.—Armor.
CARLE.—Man, hero.
EARL.—Nobleman, any brave man.
EKE.—Also.
EMPRISE.—Enterprise, undertaking.
ERST.—Formerly.
ERST-WORTHY.—Worthy for a long time past.
FAIN.—Glad.
FERRY.—Bear, carry.
FEY.—Fated, doomed.
FLOAT.—Vessel, ship.
FOIN.—To lunge (Shaks.).
GLORY OF KINGS.—God.
GREWSOME.—Cruel, fierce.
HEFT.—Handle, hilt; used by synecdoche for 'sword.'
HELM.—Helmet, protector.
HENCHMAN.—Retainer, vassal.
HIGHT.—Am (was) named.
HOLM.—Ocean, curved surface of the sea.
HIMSEEMED.—(It) seemed to him.
LIEF.—Dear, valued.
MERE.—Sea; in compounds, 'mere-ways,' 'mere-currents,' etc.
MICKLE.—Much.
NATHLESS.—Nevertheless.
NAZE.—Edge (nose).
NESS.—Edge.
NICKER.—Sea-beast.
QUIT, QUITE.—Requite.
RATHE.—Quickly.
REAVE.—Bereave, deprive.

SAIL-ROAD.—Sea.
SETTLE.—Seat, bench.
SKINKER.—One who pours.
SOOTHLY.—Truly.
SWINGE.—Stroke, blow.
TARGE, TARGET.—Shield.
THROUGHLY.—Thoroughly.
TOLD.—Counted.
UNCANNY.—Ill-featured, grizzly.
UNNETHE.—Difficult.
WAR-SPEED.—Success in war.
WEB.—Tapestry (that which is 'woven').
WEEDED.—Clad (cf. widow's weeds).
WEEN.—Suppose, imagine.
WEIRD.—Fate, Providence.
WHILOM.—At times, formerly, often.
WIELDER.—Ruler. Often used of God; also in compounds, as
  'Wielder of Glory,' 'Wielder of Worship.'
WIGHT.—Creature.
WOLD.—Plane, extended surface.
WOT.—Knows.
YOUNKER.—Youth.

I.
The Life and Death of Scyld

Lo! the Spear-Danes' glory through
    splendid achievements
The folk-kings' former fame we have
    heard of,
How princes displayed then their
    prowess-in-battle.
Oft Scyld the Scefing from scathers
    in numbers

5   From many a people their mead-
    benches tore.
Since first he found him friendless
    and wretched,
The earl had had terror: comfort he
    got for it,
Waxed 'neath the welkin, world-
    honor gained,
Till all his neighbors o'er sea were
    compelled to

10   Bow to his bidding and bring him
    their tribute:
An excellent atheling! After was
    borne him
A son and heir, young in his
    dwelling,
Whom God-Father sent to solace the
    people.
He had marked the misery malice had
    caused them,

15   [2]That reaved of their rulers they
    wretched had erstwhile[3]
Long been afflicted. The Lord, in
    requital,
Wielder of Glory, with world-honor
    blessed him.

The famous race of Spear-Danes.

Scyld, their mighty king, in honor of whom they are often called Scyldings. He is the great-grandfather of Hrothgar, so prominent in the poem.

A son is born to him, who receives the name of Beowulf—a name afterwards made so famous by the hero of the poem.

---

[2] For the 'Þæt' of verse 15, Sievers suggests 'Þá' (= which). If this be accepted, the sentence 'He had … afflicted' will read: *He (i.e.* God) *had perceived the malice-caused sorrow which they, lordless, had formerly long endured.*

[3] For 'aldor-léase' (15) Gr. suggested 'aldor-ceare': *He perceived their distress, that they formerly had suffered life-sorrow a long while.*

Famed was Beowulf, far spread the
  glory
Of Scyld's great son in the lands of
  the Danemen.

20 So the carle that is young, by
    kindnesses rendered
The friends of his father, with fees in
  abundance
Must be able to earn that when age
  approacheth
Eager companions aid him
  requitingly,
When war assaults him serve him as
  liegemen:

25 By praise-worthy actions must honor
    be got
'Mong all of the races. At the hour
  that was fated
Scyld then departed to the All-
  Father's keeping
Warlike to wend him; away then they
  bare him
To the flood of the current, his fond-
  loving comrades,

30 As himself he had bidden, while the
    friend of the Scyldings
Word-sway wielded, and the well-
  lovèd land-prince
Long did rule them.[4] The ring-
  stemmèd vessel,
Bark of the atheling, lay there at
  anchor,
Icy in glimmer and eager for sailing;

35 The belovèd leader laid they down
    there,
Giver of rings, on the breast of the
  vessel,

The ideal Teutonic king lavishes gifts on his vassals.

Scyld dies at the hour appointed by Fate.

By his own request, his body is laid on a vessel and wafted seaward.

---

[4] A very difficult passage. 'Áhte' (31) has no object. H. supplies 'geweald' from the context; and our translation is based upon this assumption, though it is far from satisfactory. Kl. suggests 'lændagas' for 'lange': *And the beloved land-prince enjoyed (had) his transitory days (i.e. lived)*. B. suggests a dislocation; but this is a dangerous doctrine, pushed rather far by that eminent scholar.

The famed by the mainmast. A many
   of jewels,
Of fretted embossings, from far-lands
   brought over,
Was placed near at hand then; and
   heard I not ever
40   That a folk ever furnished a float
   more superbly
With weapons of warfare, weeds for
   the battle,
Bills and burnies; on his bosom
   sparkled
Many a jewel that with him must
   travel
On the flush of the flood afar on the
   current.
45   And favors no fewer they furnished
   him soothly,
Excellent folk-gems, than others had
   given him
Who when first he was born outward
   did send him
Lone on the main, the merest of
   infants:
And a gold-fashioned standard they
   stretched under heaven
50   High o'er his head, let the holm-
   currents bear him,
Seaward consigned him: sad was
   their spirit,
Their mood very mournful. Men are
   not able
Soothly to tell us, they in halls who
   reside,[5]
Heroes under heaven, to what haven
   he hied.

He leaves Daneland on the breast of a bark.

No one knows whither the boat drifted.

---

[5] The reading of the H.-So. text has been quite closely followed; but some eminent scholars read 'séle-rædenne' for 'sele-rædende.' If that be adopted, the passage will read: *Men cannot tell us, indeed, the order of Fate, etc.* 'Sele-rædende' has two things to support it: (1) v. 1347; (2) it affords a parallel to 'men' in v. 50.

II.
SCYLD'S SUCCESSORS.—HROTHGAR'S GREAT MEAD-HALL.

In the boroughs then Beowulf, bairn
    of the Scyldings,

Beowulf succeeds
his father Scyld.

Belovèd land-prince, for long-lasting
    season
Was famed mid the folk (his father
    departed,
The prince from his dwelling), till
    afterward sprang

5   Great-minded Healfdene; the Danes
      in his lifetime

Healfdene's birth.

He graciously governed, grim-
    mooded, agèd.
Four bairns of his body born in
    succession
Woke in the world, war-troopers'
    leader
Heorogar, Hrothgar, and Halga the
    good;

10   Heard I that Elan was Ongentheow's
      consort,

He has three
sons—one of
them, Hrothgar—
and a daughter
named Elan.
Hrothgar becomes
a mighty king.

The well-beloved bedmate of the
    War-Scylfing leader.
Then glory in battle to Hrothgar was
    given,
Waxing of war-fame, that willingly
    kinsmen
Obeyed his bidding, till the boys grew
    to manhood,

15   A numerous band. It burned in his
      spirit

He is eager to
build a great hall
in which he may
feast his retainers.

To urge his folk to found a great
    building,
A mead-hall grander than men of the
    era
Ever had heard of, and in it to share
With young and old all of the
    blessings

20   The Lord had allowed him, save life
    and retainers.

Then the work I find afar was
    assigned
To many races in middle-earth's
    regions,
To adorn the great folk-hall. In due
    time it happened
Early 'mong men, that 'twas finished
    entirely,
25   The greatest of hall-buildings; Heorot
    he named it
Who wide-reaching word-sway
    wielded 'mong earlmen.
His promise he brake not, rings he
    lavished,
Treasure at banquet. Towered the hall
    up
High and horn-crested, huge between
    antlers:
30   It battle-waves bided, the blasting
    fire-demon;
Ere long then from hottest hatred
    must sword-wrath
Arise for a woman's husband and
    father.
Then the mighty war-spirit[6] endured
    for a season,
Bore it bitterly, he who bided in
    darkness,
35   That light-hearted laughter loud in the
    building
Greeted him daily; there was dulcet
    harp-music,
Clear song of the singer. He said that
    was able
To tell from of old earthmen's
    beginnings,
That Father Almighty earth had
    created,
40   The winsome wold that the water
    encircleth,
Set exultingly the sun's and the
    moon's beams

The hall is completed, and is called Heort, or Heorot.

The Monster Grendel is madly envious of the Danemen's joy.

[The course of the story is interrupted by a short reference to some old account of the creation.]

---

[6] R. and t. B. prefer 'ellor-gæst' to 'ellen-gæst' (86): *Then the stranger from afar endured, etc.*

To lavish their lustre on land-folk and
   races,
And earth He embellished in all her
   regions
With limbs and leaves; life He
   bestowed too
45   On all the kindreds that live under
   heaven.

> The glee of the warriors is overcast by a horrible dread.

So blessed with abundance, brimming
   with joyance,
The warriors abided, till a certain one
   gan to
Dog them with deeds of direfullest
   malice,
A foe in the hall-building: this
   horrible stranger[7]
50   Was Grendel entitled, the march-
   stepper famous
Who[8] dwelt in the moor-fens, the
   marsh and the fastness;
The wan-mooded being abode for a
   season
In the land of the giants, when the
   Lord and Creator
Had banned him and branded. For that
   bitter murder,
55   The killing of Abel, all-ruling Father

> Cain is referred to as a progenitor of Grendel, and of monsters in general.

The kindred of Cain crushed with His
   vengeance;
In the feud He rejoiced not, but far
   away drove him
From kindred and kind, that crime to
   atone for,
Meter of Justice. Thence ill-favored
   creatures,
60   Elves and giants, monsters of ocean,
Came into being, and the giants that
   longtime
Grappled with God; He gave them
   requital.

---

[7] Some authorities would translate '*demon*' instead of '*stranger.*'

[8] Some authorities arrange differently, and render: *Who dwelt in the moor-fens, the marsh and the fastness, the land of the giant-race.*

III.

Grendel the Murderer

<table>
<tr><td></td><td>When the sun was sunken, he set out to visit
The lofty hall-building, how the Ring-Danes had used it
For beds and benches when the banquet was over.
Then he found there reposing many a noble</td><td>Grendel attacks the sleeping heroes.</td></tr>
<tr><td>5</td><td>Asleep after supper; sorrow the heroes,[9]
Misery knew not. The monster of evil
Greedy and cruel tarried but little,
Fell and frantic, and forced from their slumbers
Thirty of thanemen; thence he departed</td><td>He drags off thirty of them, and devours them.</td></tr>
<tr><td>10</td><td>Leaping and laughing, his lair to return to,
With surfeit of slaughter sallying homeward.
In the dusk of the dawning, as the day was just breaking,
Was Grendel's prowess revealed to the warriors:
Then, his meal-taking finished, a moan was uplifted,</td><td>A cry of agony goes up, when Grendel's horrible deed is fully realized.</td></tr>
<tr><td>15</td><td>Morning-cry mighty. The man-ruler famous,
The long-worthy atheling, sat very woful,
Suffered great sorrow, sighed for his liegemen,
When they had seen the track of the hateful pursuer,
The spirit accursèd: too crushing that sorrow,</td><td>The monster returns the next night.</td></tr>
</table>

[9] The translation is based on 'weras,' adopted by H.-So.—K. and Th. read 'wera' and, arranging differently, render 119(2)-120: *They knew not sorrow, the wretchedness of man, aught of misfortune.*—For 'unhælo' (120) R. suggests 'unfælo': *The uncanny creature, greedy and cruel, etc.*

20 Too loathsome and lasting. Not
        longer he tarried,
    But one night after continued his
        slaughter
    Shameless and shocking, shrinking
        but little
    From malice and murder; they
        mastered him fully.
    He was easy to find then who
        otherwhere looked for
25 A pleasanter place of repose in the
        lodges,
    A bed in the bowers. Then was
        brought to his notice
    Told him truly by token apparent
    The hall-thane's hatred: he held
        himself after
    Further and faster who the foeman
        did baffle.
30 [10]So ruled he and strongly strove
        against justice
    Lone against all men, till empty
        uptowered
    The choicest of houses. Long was the
        season:
    Twelve-winters' time torture suffered
    The friend of the Scyldings, every
        affliction,
35 Endless agony; hence it
        after[11] became
    Certainly known to the children of
        men
    Sadly in measures, that long against
        Hrothgar
    Grendel struggled:—his grudges he
        cherished,
    Murderous malice, many a winter,

King Hrothgar's agony and suspense last twelve years.

---

[10] S. rearranges and translates: *So he ruled and struggled unjustly, one against all, till the noblest of buildings stood useless (it was a long while) twelve years' time: the friend of the Scyldings suffered distress, every woe, great sorrows, etc.*

[11] For 'syððan,' B. suggests 'sárcwidum': *Hence in mournful words it became well known, etc.* Various other words beginning with 's' have been conjectured.

<table>
<tr><td>40</td><td>Strife unremitting, and peacefully wished he</td><td>Grendel is unremitting in his persecutions.</td></tr>
</table>

40	Strife unremitting, and peacefully wished he	Grendel is unremitting in his persecutions.
	[12]Life-woe to lift from no liegeman at all of	
	The men of the Dane-folk, for money to settle,	
	No counsellor needed count for a moment	
	On handsome amends at the hands of the murderer;	
45	The monster of evil fiercely did harass,	
	The ill-planning death-shade, both elder and younger,	
	Trapping and tricking them. He trod every night then	
	The mist-covered moor-fens; men do not know where	
	Witches and wizards wander and ramble.	
50	So the foe of mankind many of evils	God is against the monster.
	Grievous injuries, often accomplished,	
	Horrible hermit; Heort he frequented,	
	Gem-bedecked palace, when night-shades had fallen	
	(Since God did oppose him, not the throne could he touch,[13]	
55	The light-flashing jewel, love of Him knew not).	The king and his council deliberate in vain. They invoke the aid of
	'Twas a fearful affliction to the friend of the Scyldings	

---

[12] The H.-So. glossary is very inconsistent in referring to this passage.— 'Sibbe' (154), which H.-So. regards as an instr., B. takes as accus., obj. of 'wolde.' Putting a comma after Deniga, he renders: *He did not desire peace with any of the Danes, nor did he wish to remove their life-woe, nor to settle for money.*

[13] Of this difficult passage the following interpretations among others are given: (1) Though Grendel has frequented Heorot as a demon, he could not become ruler of the Danes, on account of his hostility to God. (2) Hrothgar was much grieved that Grendel had not appeared before his throne to receive presents. (3) He was not permitted to devastate the hall, on account of the Creator; *i.e.* God wished to make his visit fatal to him.— Ne … wisse (169) W. renders: *Nor had he any desire to do so*; 'his' being obj. gen. = danach.

Soul-crushing sorrow. Not seldom in
   private
Sat the king in his council;
   conference held they
What the braves should determine
   'gainst terrors unlooked for.
60   At the shrines of their idols often they
   promised
Gifts and offerings, earnestly prayed
   they
The devil from hell would help them
   to lighten
Their people's oppression. Such
   practice they used then,
Hope of the heathen; hell they
   remembered
65   In innermost spirit, God they knew
   not,
Judge of their actions, All-wielding
   Ruler,
No praise could they give the
   Guardian of Heaven,
The Wielder of Glory. Woe will be
   his who
Through furious hatred his spirit shall
   drive to
70   The clutch of the fire, no comfort
   shall look for,
Wax no wiser; well for the man who,
Living his life-days, his Lord may
   face
And find defence in his Father's
   embrace!

IV.
Beowulf Goes to Hrothgar's Assistance

So Healfdene's kinsman constantly mused on
His long-lasting sorrow; the battle-thane clever
Was not anywise able evils to 'scape from:
Too crushing the sorrow that came to the people,

Hrothgar sees no way of escape from the persecutions of Grendel.

5   Loathsome and lasting the life-grinding torture,
Greatest of night-woes. So Higelac's liegeman,
Good amid Geatmen, of Grendel's achievements
Heard in his home:[14] of heroes then living
He was stoutest and strongest, sturdy and noble.

Beowulf, the Geat, hero of the poem, hears of Hrothgar's sorrow, and resolves to go to his assistance.

10   He bade them prepare him a bark that was trusty;
He said he the war-king would seek o'er the ocean,
The folk-leader noble, since he needed retainers.
For the perilous project prudent companions
Chided him little, though loving him dearly;

15   They egged the brave atheling, augured him glory.
The excellent knight from the folk of the Geatmen
Had liegemen selected, likest to prove them

With fourteen carefully chosen companions, he sets out for Dane-land.

---

[14] 'From hám' (194) is much disputed. One rendering is: *Beowulf, being away from home, heard of Hrothgar's troubles, etc.* Another, that adopted by S. and endorsed in the H.-So. notes, is: *B. heard from his neighborhood (neighbors), i.e. in his home, etc.* A third is: *B., being at home, heard this as occurring away from home.* The H.-So. glossary and notes conflict

Trustworthy warriors; with fourteen
   companions
The vessel he looked for; a liegeman
   then showed them,
20   A sea-crafty man, the bounds of the
   country.
Fast the days fleeted; the float was a-
   water,
The craft by the cliff. Clomb to the
   prow then
Well-equipped warriors: the wave-
   currents twisted
The sea on the sand; soldiers then
   carried
25   On the breast of the vessel bright-
   shining jewels,
Handsome war-armor; heroes
   outshoved then,
Warmen the wood-ship, on its
   wished-for adventure.
The foamy-necked floater fanned by
   the breeze,
Likest a bird, glided the waters,
30   Till twenty and four hours thereafter
The twist-stemmed vessel had
   traveled such distance
That the sailing-men saw the sloping
   embankments,
The sea cliffs gleaming, precipitous
   mountains,
Nesses enormous: they were nearing
   the limits
35   At the end of the ocean.[15] Up thence
   quickly
The men of the Weders clomb to the
   mainland,
Fastened their vessel (battle weeds
   rattled,
War burnies clattered), the Wielder
   they thanked

The vessel sails like a bird. In twenty four hours they reach the shores of Hrothgar's dominions.

They are hailed by the Danish coast guard40

---

[15] 'Eoletes' (224) is marked with a (?) by H.-So.; our rendering simply follows his conjecture.—Other conjectures as to 'eolet' are: (1) *voyage*, (2) *toil, labor*, (3) *hasty journey*.

That the ways o'er the waters had
    waxen so gentle.
40   Then well from the cliff edge the
    guard of the Scyldings
Who the sea-cliffs should see to, saw
    o'er the gangway
Brave ones bearing beauteous
    targets,
Armor all ready, anxiously thought
    he,
Musing and wondering what men
    were approaching.
45   High on his horse then Hrothgar's   His challenge
    retainer
Turned him to coastward, mightily
    brandished
His lance in his hands, questioned
    with boldness.
"Who are ye men here, mail-covered
    warriors
Clad in your corslets, come thus a-
    driving
50   A high riding ship o'er the shoals of
    the waters,
[16]And hither 'neath helmets have
    hied o'er the ocean?
I have been strand-guard, standing as
    warden,
Lest enemies ever anywise ravage
Danish dominions with army of war-
    ships.
55   More boldly never have warriors   He is struck by
    ventured   Beowulf's

---

[16] The lacuna of the MS at this point has been supplied by various conjectures. The reading adopted by H.-So. has been rendered in the above translation. W., like H.-So., makes 'ic' the beginning of a new sentence, but, for 'helmas bæron,' he reads 'hringed stefnan.' This has the advantage of giving a parallel to 'brontne ceol' instead of a kenning for 'go.'—B puts the (?) after 'holmas', and begins a new sentence at the middle of the line. Translate: *What warriors are ye, clad in armor, who have thus come bringing the foaming vessel over the water way, hither over the seas? For some time on the wall I have been coast guard, etc.* S. endorses most of what B. says, but leaves out 'on the wall' in the last sentence. If W.'s 'hringed stefnan' be accepted, change line 51 above to, *A ring-stemmed vessel hither o'ersea.*

Hither to come; of kinsmen's approval,
Word-leave of warriors, I ween that ye surely
Nothing have known. Never a greater one
Of earls o'er the earth have *I* had a sight of

appearance.

60 Than is one of your number, a hero in armor;
No low-ranking fellow[17] adorned with his weapons,
But launching them little, unless looks are deceiving,
And striking appearance. Ere ye pass on your journey
As treacherous spies to the land of the Scyldings
65 And farther fare, I fully must know now
What race ye belong to. Ye far-away dwellers,
Sea-faring sailors, my simple opinion
Hear ye and hearken: haste is most fitting
Plainly to tell me what place ye are come from."

---

[17] 'Seld-guma' (249) is variously rendered: (1) *housecarle*; (2) *home-stayer*; (3) *common man*. Dr. H. Wood suggests *a man-at-arms in another's house.*

V.
The Geats Reach Heorot

The chief of the strangers rendered him answer,
War-troopers' leader, and word-treasure opened:
"We are sprung from the lineage of the people of Geatland,
And Higelac's hearth-friends. To heroes unnumbered

Beowulf courteously replies. We are Geats.

5 My father was known, a noble head-warrior
Ecgtheow titled; many a winter
He lived with the people, ere he passed on his journey,
Old from his dwelling; each of the counsellors
Widely mid world-folk well remembers him.

My father Ecgtheow was well-known in his day.

10 We, kindly of spirit, the lord of thy people,
The son of King Healfdene, have come here to visit,
Folk-troop's defender: be free in thy counsels!
To the noble one bear we a weighty commission,
The helm of the Danemen; we shall hide, I ween,

Our intentions towards King Hrothgar are of the kindest.

15 Naught of our message. Thou know'st if it happen,
As we soothly heard say, that some savage despoiler,
Some hidden pursuer, on nights that are murky
By deeds very direful 'mid the Danemen exhibits
Hatred unheard of, horrid destruction

Is it true that a monster is slaying Danish heroes?

20 And the falling of dead. From feelings least selfish
I am able to render counsel to Hrothgar,

I can help your king to free himself from this horrible creature.

How he, wise and worthy, may worst
    the destroyer,
If the anguish of sorrow should ever
    be lessened,[18]
Comfort come to him, and care-
    waves grow cooler,
25   Or ever hereafter he agony suffer
And troublous distress, while
    towereth upward
The handsomest of houses high on
    the summit."
Bestriding his stallion, the strand-
    watchman answered,
The doughty retainer: "The
    difference surely
30   'Twixt words and works, the warlike
    shield-bearer
Who judgeth wisely well shall
    determine.
This band, I hear, beareth no malice
To the prince of the Scyldings. Pass
    ye then onward
With weapons and armor. I shall lead
    you in person;
35   To my war-trusty vassals command I
    shall issue
To keep from all injury your
    excellent vessel,
Your fresh-tarred craft, 'gainst every
    opposer
Close by the sea-shore, till the
    curved-neckèd bark shall
Waft back again the well-beloved
    hero
40   O'er the way of the water to Weder
    dominions.
To warrior so great 'twill be granted
    sure
In the storm of strife to stand
    secure."
Onward they fared then (the vessel

The coast-guard reminds Beowulf that it is easier to say than to do.

I am satisfied of your good intentions, and shall lead you to the palace.

Your boat shall be well cared for during your stay here.

He again compliments Beowulf.

---

[18] 'Edwendan' (280) B. takes to be the subs. 'edwenden' (cf. 1775); and 'bisigu' he takes as gen. sing., limiting 'edwenden': *If reparation for sorrows is ever to come.* This is supported by t.B.

<table>
<tr><td>

lay quiet,
The broad-bosomed bark was bound
    by its cable,

</td><td></td></tr>
<tr><td>

45   Firmly at anchor); the boar-signs
      glistened[19]

</td><td>

The land is
perhaps rolling.

</td></tr>
</table>

lay quiet,
The broad-bosomed bark was bound
    by its cable,
45   Firmly at anchor); the boar-signs
      glistened[19]
Bright on the visors vivid with
    gilding,
Blaze-hardened, brilliant; the boar
    acted warden.
The heroes hastened, hurried the
    liegemen,
Descended together, till they saw the
    great palace,
50   The well-fashioned wassail-hall
      wondrous and gleaming:
'Mid world-folk and kindreds that
    was widest reputed
Of halls under heaven which the hero
    abode in;
Its lustre enlightened lands without
    number.
Then the battle-brave hero showed
    them the glittering
55   Court of the bold ones, that they
      easily thither
Might fare on their journey; the
    aforementioned warrior
Turning his courser, quoth as he left
    them:
"'Tis time I were faring; Father
    Almighty
Grant you His grace, and give you to
    journey
60   Safe on your mission! To the sea I
      will get me
'Gainst hostile warriors as warden to
    stand."

Heorot flashes on their view. (line 50)

The coast-guard, having discharged his duty, bids them God-speed. (line 55)

---

[19] Combining the emendations of B. and t.B., we may read: *The boar-images glistened ... brilliant, protected the life of the war-mooded man.* They read 'ferh-wearde' (305) and 'gúðmódgum men' (306).

VI.
Beowulf Introduces Himself at the Palace

<table>
<tr><td></td><td>The highway glistened with many-
    hued pebble,</td><td></td></tr>
<tr><td></td><td>A by-path led the liegemen together.</td><td></td></tr>
<tr><td></td><td>[20]Firm and hand-locked the war-
    burnie glistened,</td><td></td></tr>
<tr><td></td><td>The ring-sword radiant rang 'mid
    the armor</td><td></td></tr>
<tr><td>5</td><td>As the party was approaching the
    palace together</td><td>They set their arms and armor against the wall.</td></tr>
<tr><td></td><td>In warlike equipments. 'Gainst the
    wall of the building</td><td></td></tr>
<tr><td></td><td>Their wide-fashioned war-shields
    they weary did set then,</td><td></td></tr>
<tr><td></td><td>Battle-shields sturdy; benchward
    they turned then;</td><td></td></tr>
<tr><td></td><td>Their battle-sarks rattled, the gear of
    the heroes;</td><td></td></tr>
<tr><td>10</td><td>The lances stood up then, all in a
    cluster,</td><td>A Danish hero asks them whence and why they are come.</td></tr>
<tr><td></td><td>The arms of the seamen, ashen-
    shafts mounted</td><td></td></tr>
<tr><td></td><td>With edges of iron: the armor-clad
    troopers</td><td></td></tr>
<tr><td></td><td>Were decked with weapons. Then a
    proud-mooded hero</td><td></td></tr>
<tr><td></td><td>Asked of the champions questions
    of lineage:</td><td></td></tr>
<tr><td>15</td><td>"From what borders bear ye your
    battle-shields plated,</td><td>He expresses no little admiration for the strangers.</td></tr>
<tr><td></td><td>Gilded and gleaming, your gray-
    colored burnies,</td><td></td></tr>
<tr><td></td><td>Helmets with visors and heap of
    war-lances?—</td><td></td></tr>
<tr><td></td><td>To Hrothgar the king I am servant
    and liegeman.</td><td></td></tr>
</table>

---

[20] Instead of the punctuation given by H.-So, S. proposed to insert a comma after 'scír' (322), and to take 'hring-íren' as meaning 'ring-mail' and as parallel with 'gúð-byrne.' The passage would then read: *The firm and hand-locked war-burnie shone, bright ring-mail, rang 'mid the armor, etc.*

'Mong folk from far-lands found I
   have never

20   Men so many of mien more
   courageous.

I ween that from valor, nowise as
   outlaws,

But from greatness of soul ye sought
   for King Hrothgar."

Then the strength-famous earlman
   answer rendered,

The proud-mooded Wederchief
   replied to his question,

25   Hardy 'neath helmet: "Higelac's
   mates are we;

Beowulf hight I. To the bairn of
   Healfdene,

The famous folk-leader, I freely will
   tell

To thy prince my commission, if
   pleasantly hearing

He'll grant we may greet him so
   gracious to all men."

30   Wulfgar replied then (he was prince
   of the Wendels,

His boldness of spirit was known
   unto many,

His prowess and prudence): "The
   prince of the Scyldings,

The friend-lord of Danemen, I will
   ask of thy journey,

The giver of rings, as thou urgest me
   do it,

35   The folk-chief famous, and inform
   thee early

What answer the good one mindeth
   to render me."

He turned then hurriedly where
   Hrothgar was sitting,

[21]Old and hoary, his earlmen
   attending him;

Beowulf replies. We are Higelac's table-companions, and bear an important commission to your prince.

Wulfgar, the thane, says that he will go and ask Hrothgar whether he will see the strangers.

---

[21] Gr. and others translate 'unhár' by 'bald'; *old and bald.*

The strength-famous went till he
   stood at the shoulder
40   Of the lord of the Danemen, of
   courteous thanemen
The custom he minded. Wulfgar
   addressed then
His friendly liegelord: "Folk of the
   Geatmen
O'er the way of the waters are
   wafted hither,
Faring from far-lands: the foremost
   in rank
45   The battle-champions Beowulf title.
They make this petition: with thee,
   O my chieftain,
To be granted a conference; O
   gracious King Hrothgar,
Friendly answer refuse not to give
   them!
In war-trappings weeded worthy
   they seem
50   Of earls to be honored; sure the
   atheling is doughty
Who headed the heroes hitherward
   coming."

He thereupon urges his liegelord to receive the visitors courteously.

Hrothgar, too, is struck with Beowulf's appearance.

VII.
Hrothgar and Beowulf

<table>
<tr><td></td><td>

Hrothgar answered, helm of the
    Scyldings:
"I remember this man as the merest
    of striplings.
His father long dead now was
    Ecgtheow titled,
Him Hrethel the Geatman granted at
    home his
</td><td>

Hrothgar remembers Beowulf as a youth, and also remembers his father.
</td></tr>
<tr><td>5</td><td>

One only daughter; his battle-brave
    son
Is come but now, sought a
    trustworthy friend.
Seafaring sailors asserted it then,
Who valuable gift-gems of the
    Geatmen[22] carried
As peace-offering thither, that he
    thirty men's grapple
</td><td>

Beowulf is reported to have the strength of thirty men.
</td></tr>
<tr><td>10</td><td>

Has in his hand, the hero-in-battle.
The holy Creator usward sent him,
To West-Dane warriors, I ween, for
    to render
'Gainst Grendel's grimness gracious
    assistance:
I shall give to the good one gift-
    gems for courage.
</td><td>

God hath sent him to our rescue.
</td></tr>
<tr><td>15</td><td>

Hasten to bid them hither to speed
    them,[23]
To see assembled this circle of
    kinsmen;
Tell them expressly they're
    welcome in sooth to
The men of the Danes." To the door
    of the building
Wulfgar went then, this word-
</td><td>

Wulfgar invites the strangers in.
</td></tr>
</table>

---

[22] Some render 'gif-sceattas' by 'tribute.'—'Géata' B. and Th. emended to 'Géatum.' If this be accepted, change '*of* the Geatmen' to '*to* the Geatmen.'

[23] If t.B.'s emendation of vv. 386, 387 be accepted, the two lines, 'Hasten … kinsmen' will read: *Hasten thou, bid the throng of kinsmen go into the hall together.*

message shouted:

20   "My victorious liegelord bade me to
      tell you,
The East-Danes' atheling, that your
      origin knows he,
And o'er wave-billows wafted ye
      welcome are hither,
Valiant of spirit. Ye straightway
      may enter
Clad in corslets, cased in your
      helmets,
25   To see King Hrothgar. Here let your
      battle-boards,
Wood-spears and war-shafts, await
      your conferring."
The mighty one rose then, with
      many a liegeman,
An excellent thane-group; some
      there did await them,
And as bid of the brave one the
      battle-gear guarded.
30   Together they hied them, while the
      hero did guide them,
'Neath Heorot's roof; the high-
      minded went then
Sturdy 'neath helmet till he stood in
      the building.
Beowulf spake (his burnie did
      glisten,
His armor seamed over by the art of
      the craftsman):
35   "Hail thou, Hrothgar! I am
      Higelac's kinsman
And vassal forsooth; many a wonder
I dared as a stripling. The doings of
      Grendel,
In far-off fatherland I fully did know
      of:
Sea-farers tell us, this hall-building
      standeth,
40   Excellent edifice, empty and useless
To all the earlmen after evenlight's
      glimmer
'Neath heaven's bright hues hath
      hidden its glory.

Beowulf salutes Hrothgar, and then proceeds to boast of his youthful achievements.

<table>
<tr><td></td><td>This my earls then urged me, the
    most excellent of them,</td><td></td></tr>
<tr><td></td><td>Carles very clever, to come and
    assist thee,</td><td></td></tr>
<tr><td>45</td><td>Folk-leader Hrothgar; fully they
    knew of</td><td>His fight with the
nickers.</td></tr>
<tr><td></td><td>The strength of my body.
    Themselves they beheld me</td><td></td></tr>
<tr><td></td><td>When I came from the contest, when
    covered with gore</td><td></td></tr>
<tr><td></td><td>Foes I escaped from, where five[24] I
    had bound,</td><td></td></tr>
<tr><td></td><td>The giant-race wasted, in the waters
    destroying</td><td></td></tr>
<tr><td>50</td><td>The nickers by night, bore
    numberless sorrows,</td><td>He intends to fight
Grendel unaided.</td></tr>
<tr><td></td><td>The Weders avenged (woes had they
    suffered)</td><td></td></tr>
<tr><td></td><td>Enemies ravaged; alone now with
    Grendel</td><td></td></tr>
<tr><td></td><td>I shall manage the matter, with the
    monster of evil,</td><td></td></tr>
<tr><td></td><td>The giant, decide it. Thee I would
    therefore</td><td></td></tr>
<tr><td>55</td><td>Beg of thy bounty, Bright-Danish
    chieftain,</td><td></td></tr>
<tr><td></td><td>Lord of the Scyldings, this single
    petition:</td><td></td></tr>
<tr><td></td><td>Not to refuse me, defender of
    warriors,</td><td></td></tr>
<tr><td></td><td>Friend-lord of folks, so far have I
    sought thee,</td><td></td></tr>
<tr><td></td><td>That *I* may unaided, my earlmen
    assisting me,</td><td></td></tr>
<tr><td>60</td><td>This brave-mooded war-band,
    purify Heorot.</td><td>Since the monster
uses no weapons,</td></tr>
</table>

---

[24] For 420 (*b*) and 421 (*a*), B. suggests: Þær ic (on) fífelgeban ýðde eotena cyn = *where I in the ocean destroyed the eoten-race.*—t.B. accepts B.'s "brilliant" 'fífelgeban,' omits 'on,' emends 'cyn' to 'hám,' arranging: Þær ic fífelgeban ýðde, eotena hám = *where I desolated the ocean, the home of the eotens.*—This would be better but for changing 'cyn' to 'hám.'—I suggest: Þær ic fífelgeband (cf. nhd. Bande) ýðde, eotena cyn = *where I conquered the monster band, the race of the eotens.* This makes no change except to read '*fífel*' for '*fífe.*'

> I have heard on inquiry, the horrible
>   creature
> From veriest rashness recks not for
>   weapons;
> I this do scorn then, so be Higelac
>   gracious,
> My liegelord belovèd, lenient of
>   spirit,

65 To bear a blade or a broad-fashioned
    target,
   A shield to the onset; only with
    hand-grip
   The foe I must grapple, fight for my
    life then,
   Foeman with foeman; he fain must
    rely on
   The doom of the Lord whom death
    layeth hold of.

I, too, shall disdain to use any. Should he crush me, he will eat my companions as he has eaten thy thanes.

70 I ween he will wish, if he win in the
    struggle,
   To eat in the war-hall earls of the
    Geat-folk,
   Boldly to swallow[25] them, as of yore
    he did often
   The best of the Hrethmen! Thou
    needest not trouble
   A head-watch to give me;[26] he will
    have me dripping

In case of my defeat, thou wilt not have the trouble of burying me.

75 And dreary with gore, if death
    overtake me,[27]

Should I fall, send my armor to my

---

[25] 'Unforhte' (444) is much disputed.—H.-So. wavers between adj. and adv. Gr. and B. take it as an adv. modifying *etan: Will eat the Geats fearlessly.*—Kl. considers this reading absurd, and proposes 'anforhte' = timid.—Understanding 'unforhte' as an adj. has this advantage, viz. that it gives a parallel to 'Geátena leóde': but to take it as an adv. is more natural. Furthermore, to call the Geats 'brave' might, at this point, seem like an implied thrust at the Danes, so long helpless; while to call his own men 'timid' would be befouling his own nest.

[26] For 'head-watch,' cf. H.-So. notes and cf. v. 2910.—Th. translates: *Thou wilt not need my head to hide* (i.e., thou wilt have no occasion to bury me, as Grendel will devour me whole).—Simrock imagines a kind of dead-watch.—Dr. H. Wood suggests: *Thou wilt not have to bury so much as my head* (for Grendel will be a thorough undertaker),—grim humor.

[27] S. proposes a colon after 'nimeð' (l. 447). This would make no essential change in the translation.

Will bear me off bleeding, biting
    and mouthing me,
The hermit will eat me, heedless of
    pity,
Marking the moor-fens; no more
    wilt thou need then
Find me my food.[28] If I fall in the
    battle,
80   Send to Higelac the armor that
    serveth
To shield my bosom, the best of
    equipments,
Richest of ring-mails; 'tis the relic
    of Hrethla,
The work of Wayland. Goes Weird
    as she must go!"

lord, King Higelac.

Weird is supreme.

---

[28] Owing to the vagueness of 'feorme' (451), this passage is variously translated. In our translation, H.-So.'s glossary has been quite closely followed. This agrees substantially with B.'s translation (P. and B. XII. 87). R. translates: *Thou needst not take care longer as to the consumption of my dead body.* 'Lic' is also a crux here, as it may mean living body or dead body

VIII.
Hrothgar and Beowulf - Continued

Hrothgar discoursed, helm of the
    Scyldings:
"To defend our folk and to furnish
    assistance,[29]
Thou soughtest us hither, good
    friend Beowulf.
The fiercest of feuds thy father
    engaged in,
5   Heatholaf killed he in hand-to-hand
    conflict
'Mid Wilfingish warriors; then the
    Wederish people
For fear of a feud were forced to
    disown him.
Thence flying he fled to the folk of
    the South-Danes,
The race of the Scyldings, o'er the
    roll of the waters;
10   I had lately begun then to govern
    the Danemen,
The hoard-seat of heroes held in
    my youth,
Rich in its jewels: dead was
    Heregar,
My kinsman and elder had earth-
    joys forsaken,
Healfdene his bairn. He was better
    than I am!
15   That feud thereafter for a fee I
    compounded;
O'er the weltering waters to the
    Wilfings I sent

Hrothgar responds. Reminiscences of Beowulf's father, Ecgtheow.

Hrothgar recounts to Beowulf the horrors of Grendel's persecutions.

---

[29] B. and S. reject the reading given in H.-So., and suggested by Grtvg. B. suggests for 457-458:

      wáere-ryhtum Þú, wine mín Béowulf,
      and for ár-stafum úsic sóhtest.

This means: *From the obligations of clientage, my friend Beowulf, and for assistance thou hast sought us.*—This gives coherence to Hrothgar's opening remarks in VIII., and also introduces a new motive for Beowulf's coming to Hrothgar's aid.

Ornaments old; oaths did he swear me.
It pains me in spirit to any to tell it,
What grief in Heorot Grendel hath caused me,

20   What horror unlooked-for, by hatred unceasing.   *My thanes have made many boasts, but have not executed them.*
Waned is my war-band, wasted my hall-troop;
Weird hath offcast them to the clutches of Grendel.
God can easily hinder the scather
From deeds so direful. Oft drunken with beer

25   O'er the ale-vessel promised warriors in armor
They would willingly wait on the wassailing-benches
A grapple with Grendel, with grimmest of edges.
Then this mead-hall at morning with murder was reeking,
The building was bloody at breaking of daylight,

30   The bench-deals all flooded, dripping and bloodied,   *Sit down to the feast, and give us comfort. A bench is made ready for Beowulf and his party.*
The folk-hall was gory: I had fewer retainers,
Dear-beloved warriors, whom death had laid hold of.
Sit at the feast now, thy intents unto heroes,[30]
Thy victor-fame show, as thy spirit doth urge thee!"

35   For the men of the Geats then together assembled,   *The gleeman sings.*

---

[30] *Sit now at the feast, and disclose thy purposes to the victorious heroes, as thy spirit urges.*—Kl. reaches the above translation by erasing the comma after 'meoto' and reading 'sige-hrèðsecgum.'—There are other and bolder emendations and suggestions. Of these the boldest is to regard 'meoto' as a verb (imperative), and read 'on sæl': *Think upon gayety, etc.*—All the renderings are unsatisfactory, the one given in our translation involving a zeugma.

In the beer-hall blithesome a bench
    was made ready;
There warlike in spirit they went to
    be seated,
Proud and exultant. A liegeman did
    service,
Who a beaker embellished bore
    with decorum,
40   And gleaming-drink poured. The   The heroes all
    gleeman sang whilom   rejoice together.
Hearty in Heorot; there was heroes'
    rejoicing,
A numerous war-band of Weders
    and Danemen.

IX.
Unferth Taunts Beowulf

Unferth spoke up, Ecglaf his son,
Who sat at the feet of the lord of the
    Scyldings,
Opened the jousting (the
    journey[31] of Beowulf,
Sea-farer doughty, gave sorrow to
    Unferth
5   And greatest chagrin, too, for
    granted he never
That any man else on earth should
    attain to,
Gain under heaven, more glory than
    he):
"Art thou that Beowulf with Breca
    did struggle,
On the wide sea-currents at
    swimming contended,
10 Where to humor your pride the
    ocean ye tried,
From vainest vaunting adventured
    your bodies
In care of the waters? And no one
    was able
Nor lief nor loth one, in the least to
    dissuade you
Your difficult voyage; then ye
    ventured a-swimming,
15 Where your arms outstretching the
    streams ye did cover,
The mere-ways measured, mixing
    and stirring them,
Glided the ocean; angry the waves
    were,
With the weltering of winter. In the
    water's possession,
Ye toiled for a seven-night; he at
    swimming outdid thee,

Sidenotes:

Unferth, a thane of Hrothgar, is jealous of Beowulf, and undertakes to twit him.

Did you take part in a swimming-match with Breca?

'Twas mere folly that actuated you both to risk your lives on the ocean.

---

[31] It has been plausibly suggested that 'síð' (in 501 and in 353) means 'arrival.' If so, translate the bracket: *(the arrival of Beowulf, the brave seafarer, was a source of great chagrin to Unferth, etc.)*.

20 In strength excelled thee. Then
   early at morning
 On the Heathoremes' shore the
   holm-currents tossed him,
 Sought he thenceward the home of
   his fathers,
 Beloved of his liegemen, the land
   of the Brondings,
 The peace-castle pleasant, where a
   people he wielded,
25 Had borough and jewels. The
   pledge that he made thee

> Breca outdid you entirely. Much more will Grendel outdo you, if you vie with him in prowess.

 The son of Beanstan hath soothly
   accomplished.
 Then I ween thou wilt find thee less
   fortunate issue,
 Though ever triumphant in onset of
   battle,
 A grim grappling, if Grendel thou
   darest
30 For the space of a night near-by to
   wait for!"

> Beowulf retaliates. O friend Unferth, you are fuddled with beer, and cannot talk coherently.

 Beowulf answered, offspring of
   Ecgtheow:
 "My good friend Unferth, sure
   freely and wildly,
 Thou fuddled with beer of Breca
   hast spoken,
 Hast told of his journey! A fact I
   allege it,
35 That greater strength in the waters I
   had then,

> We simply kept an engagement made in early life.

 Ills in the ocean, than any man else
   had.
 We made agreement as the merest
   of striplings
 Promised each other (both of us
   then were
 Younkers in years) that we yet
   would adventure
40 Out on the ocean; it all we
   accomplished.

> He *could* not excel me, and I *would* not excel him.

 While swimming the sea-floods,
   sword-blade unscabbarded

Boldly we brandished, our bodies expected
    To shield from the sharks. He sure was unable
    To swim on the waters further than I could,

45   More swift on the waves, nor *would* I from him go.

    Then we two companions stayed in the ocean
    Five nights together, till the currents did part us,
    The weltering waters, weathers the bleakest,
    And nethermost night, and the north-wind whistled

50   Fierce in our faces; fell were the billows.

    The mere fishes' mood was mightily ruffled:
    And there against foemen my firm-knotted corslet,
    Hand-jointed, hardy, help did afford me;
    My battle-sark braided, brilliantly gilded,

55   Lay on my bosom. To the bottom then dragged me,
    A hateful fiend-scather, seized me and held me,
    Grim in his grapple: 'twas granted me, nathless,
    To pierce the monster with the point of my weapon,
    My obedient blade; battle offcarried

60   The mighty mere-creature by means of my hand-blow.

After five days the currents separated us.

A horrible sea-beast attacked me, but I slew him.

X.

Beowulf Silences Unferth – Glee is High

"So ill-meaning enemies often did cause me
Sorrow the sorest. I served them, in quittance,
With my dear-lovèd sword, as in sooth it was fitting;
They missed the pleasure of feasting abundantly,

My dear sword always served me faithfully.

5 Ill-doers evil, of eating my body,
Of surrounding the banquet deep in the ocean;
But wounded with edges early at morning
They were stretched a-high on the strand of the ocean,
Put to sleep with the sword, that sea-going travelers

I put a stop to the outrages of the sea-monsters.

10 No longer thereafter were hindered from sailing
The foam-dashing currents. Came a light from the east,
God's beautiful beacon; the billows subsided,
That well I could see the nesses projecting,
The blustering crags. Weird often saveth

Fortune helps the brave earl.

15 The undoomed hero if doughty his valor!
But me did it fortune[32] to fell with my weapon
Nine of the nickers. Of night-struggle harder
'Neath dome of the heaven heard I but rarely,
Nor of wight more woful in the waves

---

[32] The repetition of 'hwæðere' (574 and 578) is regarded by some scholars as a defect. B. suggests 'swá þær' for the first: *So there it befell me, etc.* Another suggestion is to change the second 'hwæðere' into 'swá þær': *So there I escaped with my life, etc.*

of the ocean;
20   Yet I 'scaped with my life the grip of
    the monsters,
   Weary from travel. Then the waters
    bare me
   To the land of the Finns, the flood
    with the current,
   The weltering waves. Not a word hath
    been told me
   Of deeds so daring done by thee,
    Unferth,
25   And of sword-terror none; never hath
    Breca
   At the play of the battle, nor either of
    you two,
   Feat so fearless performèd with
    weapons
   Glinting and gleaming . . . .
   . . . . I utter no boasting;
30   Though with cold-blooded cruelty
    thou killedst thy brothers,
   Thy nearest of kin; thou needs must in
    hell get
   Direful damnation, though doughty
    thy wisdom.
   I tell thee in earnest, offspring of
    Ecglaf,
   Never had Grendel such numberless
    horrors,
35   The direful demon, done to thy
    liegelord,
   Harrying in Heorot, if thy heart were
    as sturdy,
   Thy mood as ferocious as thou dost
    describe them.
   He hath found out fully that the fierce-
    burning hatred,
   The edge-battle eager, of all of your
    kindred,
40   Of the Victory-Scyldings, need little
    dismay him:
   Oaths he exacteth, not any he spares
   Of the folk of the Danemen, but
    fighteth with pleasure,
   Killeth and feasteth, no contest

Marginal glosses:

After that escape I drifted to Finland. I have never heard of your doing any such bold deeds.

You are a slayer of brothers, and will suffer damnation, wise as you may be.

Had your acts been as brave as your words, Grendel had not ravaged your land so long.

The monster is not afraid of the Danes, but he will soon learn to dread the Geats.

expecteth
From Spear-Danish people. But the
   prowess and valor
45   Of the earls of the Geatmen early shall
   venture
To give him a grapple. He shall go
   who is able
Bravely to banquet, when the bright-
   light of morning
Which the second day bringeth, the
   sun in its ether-robes,
O'er children of men shines from the
   southward!"
50   Then the gray-haired, war-famed
   giver of treasure
Was blithesome and joyous, the
   Bright-Danish ruler
Expected assistance; the people's
   protector
Heard from Beowulf his bold
   resolution.
There was laughter of heroes; loud
   was the clatter,
55   The words were winsome.
   Wealhtheow advanced then,
Consort of Hrothgar, of courtesy
   mindful,
Gold-decked saluted the men in the
   building,
And the freeborn woman the beaker
   presented
To the lord of the kingdom, first of the
   East-Danes,
60   Bade him be blithesome when beer
   was a-flowing,
Lief to his liegemen; he lustily tasted
Of banquet and beaker, battle-famed
   ruler.
The Helmingish lady then graciously
   circled
'Mid all the liegemen lesser and
   greater:
65   Treasure-cups tendered, till time was
   afforded
That the decorous-mooded, diademed

Marginal notes:

On the second day, any warrior may go unmolested to the mead-banquet.

Hrothgar's spirits are revived. The old king trusts Beowulf. The heroes are joyful.

Queen Wealhtheow plays the hostess. She offers the cup to her husband first.

She gives presents to the heroes.

Then she offers the cup to Beowulf,

folk-queen

thanking God that aid has come.

Might bear to Beowulf the bumper
   o'errunning;
She greeted the Geat-prince, God she
   did thank,
Most wise in her words, that her wish
   was accomplished,
70   That in any of earlmen she ever
   should look for

Beowulf states to the queen the object of his visit.

Solace in sorrow. He accepted the
   beaker,
Battle-bold warrior, at Wealhtheow's
   giving,
Then equipped for combat quoth he in
   measures,
Beowulf spake, offspring of
   Ecgtheow:
75   "I purposed in spirit when I mounted
   the ocean,

I determined to do or die.

When I boarded my boat with a band
   of my liegemen,
I would work to the fullest the will of
   your people
Or in foe's-clutches fastened fall in
   the battle.
Deeds I shall do of daring and
   prowess,
80   Or the last of my life-days live in this
   mead-hall."

Glee is high.

These words to the lady were
   welcome and pleasing,
The boast of the Geatman; with gold
   trappings broidered
Went the freeborn folk-queen her
   fond-lord to sit by.
Then again as of yore was heard in the
   building
85   Courtly discussion, conquerors'
   shouting,
Heroes were happy, till Healfdene's
   son would
Go to his slumber to seek for
   refreshing;
For the horrid hell-monster in the hall-
   building knew he

A fight was determined,[33] since the
    light of the sun they
90   No longer could see, and lowering
    darkness
    O'er all had descended, and dark
    under heaven
    Shadowy shapes came shying around
    them.
    The liegemen all rose then. One
    saluted the other,
    Hrothgar Beowulf, in rhythmical
    measures,
95   Wishing him well, and, the wassail-
    hall giving
    To his care and keeping, quoth he
    departing:
    "Not to any one else have I ever
    entrusted,
    But thee and thee only, the hall of the
    Danemen,
    Since high I could heave my hand and
    my buckler.
100   Take thou in charge now the noblest
    of houses;
    Be mindful of honor, exhibiting
    prowess,
    Watch 'gainst the foeman! Thou shalt
    want no enjoyments,
    Survive thou safely adventure so
    glorious!"

Hrothgar retires, leaving Beowulf in charge of the hall.

---

[33] Kl. suggests a period after 'determined.' This would give the passage as follows: *Since they no longer could see the light of the sun, and lowering darkness was down over all, dire under the heavens shadowy beings came going around them.*

XI.
All Sleep Save One

Then Hrothgar departed, his earl-
  throng attending him,
Folk-lord of Scyldings, forth from
  the building;
The war-chieftain wished then
  Wealhtheow to look for,
The queen for a bedmate. To keep
  away Grendel

5 The Glory of Kings had given a
    hall-watch,
As men heard recounted: for the
  king of the Danemen
He did special service, gave the
  giant a watcher:
And the prince of the Geatmen
  implicitly trusted
His warlike strength and the
  Wielder's protection.

10 His armor of iron off him he did
    then,
His helmet from his head, to his
  henchman committed
His chased-handled chain-sword,
  choicest of weapons,
And bade him bide with his battle-
  equipments.
The good one then uttered words of
  defiance,

15 Beowulf Geatman, ere his bed he
    upmounted:
"I hold me no meaner in matters of
  prowess,
In warlike achievements, than
  Grendel does himself;
Hence I seek not with sword-edge
  to sooth him to slumber,
Of life to bereave him, though well
  I am able.

Hrothgar retires. God has provided a watch for the hall.

Beowulf is self-confident. He prepares for rest.

Beowulf boasts of his ability to cope with Grendel.

20   No battle-skill[34] has he, that blows
      he should strike me,
   To shatter my shield, though sure he
      is mighty
   In strife and destruction; but
      struggling by night we
   Shall do without edges, dare he to
      look for
   Weaponless warfare, and wise-
      mooded Father

We will fight with nature's weapons only.

25   The glory apportion, God ever-holy,
   On which hand soever to him
      seemeth proper."
   Then the brave-mooded hero bent to
      his slumber,
   The pillow received the cheek of the
      noble;
   And many a martial mere-thane
      attending

God may decide who shall conquer. The Geatish warriors lie down.

30   Sank to his slumber. Seemed it
      unlikely
   That ever thereafter any should
      hope to
   Be happy at home, hero-friends visit
   Or the lordly troop-castle where he
      lived from his childhood;
   They had heard how slaughter had
      snatched from the wine-hall,

They thought it very unlikely that they should ever see their homes again.

35   Had recently ravished, of the race of
      the Scyldings
   Too many by far. But the Lord to
      them granted
   The weaving of war-speed, to
      Wederish heroes
   Aid and comfort, that every
      opponent
   By one man's war-might they
      worsted and vanquished,

But God raised up a deliverer. God rules the world.

40   By the might of himself; the truth is
      established
   That God Almighty hath governed

Grendel comes to Heorot. Only one warrior is awake.

---

[34] Gr. understood 'gódra' as meaning 'advantages in battle.' This rendering H.-So. rejects. The latter takes the passage as meaning that Grendel, though mighty and formidable, has no skill in the art of war.

for ages

Kindreds and nations. A night very
lurid

The trav'ler-at-twilight came
tramping and striding.

The warriors were sleeping who
should watch the horned-
building,

45   One only excepted. 'Mid earthmen
'twas 'stablished,

Th' implacable foeman was
powerless to hurl them

To the land of shadows, if the Lord
were unwilling;

But serving as warder, in terror to
foemen,

He angrily bided the issue of
battle.[35]

---

[35] B. in his masterly articles on Beowulf (P. and B. XII.) rejects the division usually made at this point, 'Þá.' (711), usually rendered 'then,' he translates 'when,' and connects its clause with the foregoing sentence. These changes he makes to reduce the number of 'cóm's' as principal verbs. (Cf. 703, 711, 721.) With all deference to this acute scholar, I must say that it seems to me that the poet is exhausting his resources to bring out clearly the supreme event on which the whole subsequent action turns. First, he (Grendel) came *in the wan night*; second, he came *from the moor*; third, he came *to the hall*. Time, place from which, place to which, are all given.

XI.

Grendel and Beowulf

'Neath the cloudy cliffs came from
   the moor then
Grendel going, God's anger bare he.
The monster intended some one of
   earthmen
In the hall-building grand to entrap
   and make way with:

  5 He went under welkin where well
   he knew of
The wine-joyous building, brilliant
   with plating,
Gold-hall of earthmen. Not the
   earliest occasion
He the home and manor of Hrothgar
   had sought:
Ne'er found he in life-days later nor
   earlier

10 Hardier hero, hall-thanes[36] more
   sturdy!
Then came to the building the
   warrior marching,
Bereft of his joyance. The door
   quickly opened
On fire-hinges fastened, when his
   fingers had touched it;
The fell one had flung then—his
   fury so bitter—

15 Open the entrance. Early thereafter
The foeman trod the shining hall-
   pavement,
Strode he angrily; from the eyes of
   him glimmered
A lustre unlovely likest to fire.
He beheld in the hall the heroes in
   numbers,

Grendel comes from the fens. He goes towards the joyous building.

This was not his first visit there.

His horrid fingers tear the door open.

He strides furiously into the hall.

---

[36] B. and t.B. emend so as to make lines 9 and 10 read: *Never in his life, earlier or later, had he, the hell-thane, found a braver hero.*—They argue that Beowulf's companions had done nothing to merit such encomiums as the usual readings allow them.

<table>
<tr><td>20</td><td>A circle of kinsmen sleeping together,
A throng of thanemen: then his thoughts were exultant,
He minded to sunder from each of the thanemen
The life from his body, horrible demon,
Ere morning came, since fate had allowed him</td><td>He exults over his supposed prey.</td></tr>
<tr><td>25</td><td>The prospect of plenty. Providence willed not
To permit him any more of men under heaven
To eat in the night-time. Higelac's kinsman
Great sorrow endured how the dire-mooded creature
In unlooked-for assaults were likely to bear him.</td><td>Fate has decreed that he shall devour no more heroes. Beowulf suffers from suspense.</td></tr>
<tr><td>30</td><td>No thought had the monster of deferring the matter,
But on earliest occasion he quickly laid hold of
A soldier asleep, suddenly tore him,
Bit his bone-prison, the blood drank in currents,
Swallowed in mouthfuls: he soon had the dead man's</td><td>Grendel immediately seizes a sleeping warrior, and devours him.</td></tr>
<tr><td>35</td><td>Feet and hands, too, eaten entirely.
Nearer he strode then, the stout-hearted warrior
Snatched as he slumbered, seizing with hand-grip,
Forward the foeman foined with his hand;
Caught he quickly the cunning deviser,</td><td>Beowulf and Grendel grapple.</td></tr>
<tr><td>40</td><td>On his elbow he rested. This early discovered
The master of malice, that in middle-earth's regions,
'Neath the whole of the heavens, no hand-grapple greater</td><td>The monster is amazed at Beowulf's strength.</td></tr>
</table>

In any man else had he ever
    encountered:
Fearful in spirit, faint-mooded
    waxed he,
45   Not off could betake him; death he
    was pondering,
Would fly to his covert, seek the
    devils' assembly:
His calling no more was the same
    he had followed
Long in his lifetime. The liege-
    kinsman worthy
Of Higelac minded his speech of
    the evening,
50   Stood he up straight and stoutly did
    seize him.
His fingers crackled; the giant was
    outward,
The earl stepped farther. The
    famous one minded
To flee away farther, if he found an
    occasion,
And off and away, avoiding delay,
55   To fly to the fen-moors; he fully
    was ware of
The strength of his grapple in the
    grip of the foeman.
'Twas an ill-taken journey that the
    injury-bringing,
Harrying harmer to Heorot
    wandered:
The palace re-echoed; to all of the
    Danemen,
60   Dwellers in castles, to each of the
    bold ones,
Earlmen, was terror. Angry they
    both were,
Archwarders raging.[37] Rattled the
    building;
'Twas a marvellous wonder that the
    wine-hall withstood then

He is anxious to flee. Beowulf recalls his boast of the evening, and determines to fulfil it.

'Twas a luckless day for Grendel. The hall groans.

---

[37] For 're̊ðe ré̊n-weardas' (771), t.B. suggests 're̊ðe, ré̊nhearde.'
Translate: *They were both angry, raging and mighty.*

> The bold-in-battle, bent not to
>   earthward,
> 65 Excellent earth-hall; but within and
>   without it
> Was fastened so firmly in fetters of
>   iron,
> By the art of the armorer. Off from
>   the sill there
> Bent mead-benches many, as men
>   have informed me,
> Adorned with gold-work, where the
>   grim ones did struggle.
> 70 The Scylding wise men weened
>   ne'er before
> That by might and main-strength a
>   man under heaven
> Might break it in pieces, bone-
>   decked, resplendent,
> Crush it by cunning, unless clutch
>   of the fire
> In smoke should consume it. The
>   sound mounted upward
> 75 Novel enough; on the North Danes
>   fastened
> A terror of anguish, on all of the
>   men there
> Who heard from the wall the
>   weeping and plaining,
> The song of defeat from the foeman
>   of heaven,
> Heard him hymns of horror howl,
>   and his sorrow
> 80 Hell-bound bewailing. He held him
>   too firmly
> Who was strongest of main-strength
>   of men of that era.

Grendel's cries terrify the Danes.

XIII.
Grendel is Vanquished

For no cause whatever would the
    earlmen's defender
Leave in life-joys the loathsome
    newcomer,
He deemed his existence utterly
    useless
To men under heaven. Many a noble

Beowulf has no idea of letting Grendel live.

5   Of Beowulf brandished his battle-
    sword old,
Would guard the life of his lord and
    protector,
The far-famous chieftain, if able to
    do so;

No weapon would harm Grendel; he bore a charmed life.

While waging the warfare, this wist
    they but little,
Brave battle-thanes, while his body
    intending
10   To slit into slivers, and seeking his
    spirit:
That the relentless foeman nor finest
    of weapons
Of all on the earth, nor any of war-
    bills
Was willing to injure; but weapons
    of victory
Swords and suchlike he had sworn
    to dispense with.
15   His death at that time must prove to
    be wretched,
And the far-away spirit widely
    should journey
Into enemies' power. This plainly he
    saw then
Who with mirth[38] of mood malice
    no little
Had wrought in the past on the race

---

[38] It has been proposed to translate 'myrðe' by *with sorrow*; but there seems
no authority for such a rendering. To the present translator, the phrase
'módes myrðe' seems a mere padding for *gladly*; i.e., *he who gladly
harassed mankind.*

of the earthmen

20 (To God he was hostile), that his
body would fail him,
But Higelac's hardy henchman and
kinsman
Held him by the hand; hateful to
other
Was each one if living. A body-
wound suffered
The direful demon, damage
incurable

25 Was seen on his shoulder, his sinews
were shivered,
His body did burst. To Beowulf was
given
Glory in battle; Grendel from
thenceward
Must flee and hide him in the fen-
cliffs and marshes,
Sick unto death, his dwelling must
look for

30 Unwinsome and woful; he wist the
more fully
The end of his earthly existence was
nearing,
His life-days' limits. At last for the
Danemen,
When the slaughter was over, their
wish was accomplished.
The comer-from-far-land had
cleansed then of evil,

35 Wise and valiant, the war-hall of
Hrothgar,
Saved it from violence. He joyed in
the night-work,
In repute for prowess; the prince of
the Geatmen
For the East-Danish people his boast
had accomplished,
Bettered their burdensome bale-
sorrows fully,

40 The craft-begot evil they erstwhile
had suffered
And were forced to endure from
crushing oppression,

Grendel is sorely
wounded. His body
bursts.

The monster flees
away to hide in the
moors.

Beowulf suspends
Grendel's hand
and arm in Heorot.

Their manifold misery. 'Twas a
    manifest token,
When the hero-in-battle the hand
    suspended,
The arm and the shoulder (there was
    all of the claw
45 Of Grendel together) 'neath great-
    stretching hall-roof.

XIV.
Rejoicing of the Danes

In the mist of the morning many a
    warrior
Stood round the gift-hall, as the
    story is told me:
Folk-princes fared then from far and
    from near
Through long-stretching journeys to
    look at the wonder,

At early dawn, warriors from far and near come together to hear of the night's adventures.

5   The footprints of the foeman. Few
       of the warriors
Who gazed on the foot-tracks of the
    inglorious creature
His parting from life pained very
    deeply,
How, weary in spirit, off from those
    regions
In combats conquered he carried his
    traces,

Few warriors lamented Grendel's destruction.

10   Fated and flying, to the flood of the
      nickers.
There in bloody billows bubbled the
    currents,
The angry eddy was everywhere
    mingled
And seething with gore, welling
    with sword-blood;[39]
He death-doomed had hid him,
    when reaved of his joyance

Grendel's blood dyes the waters.

15   He laid down his life in the lair he
      had fled to,
His heathenish spirit, where hell did
    receive him.
Thence the friends from of old
    backward turned them,
And many a younker from merry

---

[39] S. emends, suggesting 'déop' for 'déog,' and removing semicolon after 'wéol.' The two half-lines 'welling ... hid him' would then read: *The bloody deep welled with sword-gore.* B. accepts 'déop' for 'déog,' but reads 'déað-fæges': *The deep boiled with the sword-gore of the death-doomed one.*

adventure,
Striding their stallions, stout from
the seaward,
20 Heroes on horses. There were heard
very often
Beowulf's praises; many often
asserted
That neither south nor north, in the
circuit of waters,
O'er outstretching earth-plain, none
other was better
'Mid bearers of war-shields, more
worthy to govern,
25 'Neath the arch of the ether. Not
any, however,
'Gainst the friend-lord muttered,
mocking-words uttered
Of Hrothgar the gracious (a good
king he).
Oft the famed ones permitted their
fallow-skinned horses
To run in rivalry, racing and
chasing,
30 Where the fieldways appeared to
them fair and inviting,
Known for their excellence; oft a
thane of the folk-lord,[40]
[41]A man of celebrity, mindful of
rhythms,
Who ancient traditions treasured in
memory,
New word-groups found properly
bound:
35 The bard after 'gan then Beowulf's
venture
Wisely to tell of, and words that
were clever

Beowulf is the hero of the hour. He is regarded as a probable successor to Hrothgar.

But no word is uttered to derogate from the old king.

The gleeman sings the deeds of heroes.

He sings in alliterative measures of Beowulf's prowess. Also of

---

[40] Another and quite different rendering of this passage is as follows: *Oft a liegeman of the king, a fame-covered man mindful of songs, who very many ancient traditions remembered (he found other word-groups accurately bound together) began afterward to tell of Beowulf's adventure, skilfully to narrate it, etc.*

[41] Might 'guma gilp-hladen' mean 'a man laden with boasts of the deeds of others'?

To utter skilfully, earnestly
  speaking,
Everything told he that he heard as
  to Sigmund's
Mighty achievements, many things
  hidden,
40   The strife of the Wælsing, the wide-
  going ventures
The children of men knew of but
  little,
The feud and the fury, but Fitela
  with him,
When suchlike matters he minded to
  speak of,
Uncle to nephew, as in every
  contention
45   Each to other was ever devoted:
A numerous host of the race of the
  scathers
They had slain with the sword-edge.
  To Sigmund accrued then
No little of glory, when his life-days
  were over,
Since he sturdy in struggle had
  destroyed the great dragon,
50   The hoard-treasure's keeper; 'neath
  the hoar-grayish stone he,
The son of the atheling, unaided
  adventured
The perilous project; not present
  was Fitela,
Yet the fortune befell him of forcing
  his weapon
Through the marvellous dragon, that
  it stood in the wall,
55   Well-honored weapon; the worm
  was slaughtered.
The great one had gained then by
  his glorious achievement
To reap from the ring-hoard richest
  enjoyment,
As best it did please him: his vessel
  he loaded,
Shining ornaments on the ship's
  bosom carried,

> Sigemund, who has slain a great fire-dragon.

<table>
<tr><td>60</td><td>Kinsman of Wæls: the drake in heat melted.
He was farthest famed of fugitive pilgrims,
Mid wide-scattered world-folk, for works of great prowess,
War-troopers' shelter: hence waxed he in honor.[42]
Afterward Heremod's hero-strength failed him,</td><td>Sigemund was widely famed. Heremod, an unfortunate Danish king, is introduced by way of contrast.</td></tr>
<tr><td>65</td><td>His vigor and valor. 'Mid venomous haters
To the hands of foemen he was foully delivered,
Offdriven early. Agony-billows
Oppressed him too long, to his people he became then,
To all the athelings, an ever-great burden;</td><td>Unlike Sigemund and Beowulf, Heremod was a burden to his people.</td></tr>
<tr><td>70</td><td>And the daring one's journey in days of yore
Many wise men were wont to deplore,
Such as hoped he would bring them help in their sorrow,
That the son of their ruler should rise into power,
Holding the headship held by his fathers,</td><td></td></tr>
<tr><td>75</td><td>Should govern the people, the gold-hoard and borough,
The kingdom of heroes, the realm of the Scyldings.
He to all men became then far more beloved,
Higelac's kinsman, to kindreds and races,
To his friends much dearer; him malice assaulted.—</td><td>Beowulf is an honor to his race. The story is resumed.</td></tr>
<tr><td>80</td><td>Oft running and racing on roadsters they measured</td><td></td></tr>
</table>

---

[42] t.B. accepts B.'s 'hé þæs áron þáh' as given by H.-So., but puts a comma after 'þáh,' and takes 'siððan' as introducing a dependent clause: *He throve in honor since Heremod's strength ... had decreased.*

The dun-colored highways. Then
    the light of the morning
Was hurried and hastened. Went
    henchmen in numbers
To the beautiful building, bold ones
    in spirit,
To look at the wonder; the liegelord
    himself then
85   From his wife-bower wending,
    warden of treasures,
Glorious trod with troopers
    unnumbered,
Famed for his virtues, and with him
    the queen-wife
Measured the mead-ways, with
    maidens attending.

XV.
Hrothgar's Gratitude

Hrothgar discoursed (to the hall-
    building went he,
He stood by the pillar,[43] saw the
    steep-rising hall-roof
Gleaming with gold-gems, and
    Grendel his hand there):
"For the sight we behold now,
    thanks to the Wielder

Hrothgar gives thanks for the overthrow of the monster.

5   Early be offered! Much evil I bided,
Snaring from Grendel:[44] God can
    e'er 'complish
Wonder on wonder, Wielder of
    Glory!

I had given up all hope, when this brave liegeman came to our aid.

But lately I reckoned ne'er under
    heaven
Comfort to gain me for any of
    sorrows,
10   While the handsomest of houses
    horrid with bloodstain
Gory uptowered; grief had
    offfrightened[45]
Each of the wise ones who weened
    not that ever
The folk-troop's defences 'gainst
    foes they should strengthen,
'Gainst sprites and monsters.
    Through the might of the Wielder
15   A doughty retainer hath a deed now
    accomplished

If his mother yet liveth, well may she thank God for this son.

Which erstwhile we all with our
    excellent wisdom
Failed to perform. May affirm very
    truly

---

[43] B. and t.B. read 'staþole,' and translate *stood on the floor*.

[44] For 'snaring from Grendel,' 'sorrows at Grendel's hands' has been suggested. This gives a parallel to 'láðes.' 'Grynna' may well be gen. pl. of 'gyrn,' by a scribal slip.

[45] The H.-So punctuation has been followed; but B. has been followed in understanding 'gehwylcne' as object of 'wíd-scofen (hæfde).' Gr. construes 'wéa' as nom abs.

What woman soever in all of the
    nations
Gave birth to the child, if yet she
    surviveth,
20   That the long-ruling Lord was
        lavish to herward
In the birth of the bairn. Now,
    Beowulf dear,
Most excellent hero, I'll love thee in
    spirit
As bairn of my body; bear well
    henceforward
The relationship new. No lack shall
    befall thee
25   Of earth-joys any I ever can give
        thee.
Full often for lesser service I've
    given
Hero less hardy hoard-treasure
    precious,
To a weaker in war-strife. By works
    of distinction
Thou hast gained for thyself now
    that thy glory shall flourish
30   Forever and ever. The All-Ruler
        quite thee
With good from His hand as He
    hitherto did thee!"
Beowulf answered, Ecgtheow's
    offspring:
"That labor of glory most gladly
    achieved we,
The combat accomplished,
    unquailing we ventured
35   The enemy's grapple; I would grant
        it much rather
Thou wert able to look at the
    creature in person,
Faint unto falling, the foe in his
    trappings!
On murder-bed quickly I minded to
    bind him,
With firm-holding fetters, that
    forced by my grapple
40   Low he should lie in life-and-death

Hereafter,
Beowulf, thou shalt
be my son.

Thou hast won
immortal
distinction.

Beowulf replies: I
was most happy to
render thee this
service.

I could not keep the

struggle
’Less his body escape; I was wholly
    unable,
Since God did not will it, to keep
    him from going,
Not held him that firmly, hated
    opposer;
Too swift was the foeman. Yet
    safety regarding

monster from escaping, as God did not will that I should.

45 He suffered his hand behind him to
    linger,
His arm and shoulder, to act as
    watcher;
No shadow of solace the woe-
    begone creature
Found him there nathless: the hated
    destroyer
Liveth no longer, lashed for his
    evils,

He left his hand and arm behind.

50 But sorrow hath seized him, in
    snare-meshes hath him
Close in its clutches, keepeth him
    writhing
In baleful bonds: there banished for
    evil
The man shall wait for the mighty
    tribunal,
How the God of glory shall give
    him his earnings.”

God will give him his deserts.

55 Then the soldier kept silent, son of
    old Ecglaf,
From boasting and bragging of
    battle-achievements,
Since the princes beheld there the
    hand that depended
’Neath the lofty hall-timbers by the
    might of the nobleman,
Each one before him, the enemy’s
    fingers;

Unferth has nothing more to say, for Beowulf’s actions speak louder than words.

60 Each finger-nail strong steel most
    resembled,
The heathen one’s hand-spur, the
    hero-in-battle’s
Claw most uncanny; quoth they
    agreeing,

No sword will harm the monster.

That not any excellent edges of
    brave ones
Was willing to touch him, the
    terrible creature's
65   Battle-hand bloody to bear away
    from him.

XVI.
Hrothgar Lavishes Gifts Upon His Deliverer

Then straight was ordered that Heorot inside[46]
    With hands be embellished: a host of them gathered,
Of men and women, who the wassailing-building
The guest-hall begeared. Gold-flashing sparkled

  5 Webs on the walls then, of wonders a many
To each of the heroes that look on such objects.
The beautiful building was broken to pieces
Which all within with irons was fastened,
Its hinges torn off: only the roof was

  10 Whole and uninjured when the horrible creature
Outlawed for evil off had betaken him,
Hopeless of living. 'Tis hard to avoid it
(Whoever will do it!); but he doubtless must come to[47]
The place awaiting, as Wyrd hath appointed,

  15 Soul-bearers, earth-dwellers, earls under heaven,
Where bound on its bed his body

Heorot is adorned with hands.

The hall is defaced, however.

[A vague passage of five verses.]

Hrothgar goes to the banquet.

---

[46] Kl. suggests 'hroden' for 'háten,' and renders: *Then quickly was Heorot adorned within, with hands bedecked.*—B. suggests 'gefrætwon' instead of 'gefrætwod,' and renders: *Then was it commanded to adorn Heorot within quickly with hands.*—The former has the advantage of affording a parallel to 'gefrætwod': both have the disadvantage of altering the text.

[47] The passage 1005-1009 seems to be hopeless. One difficult point is to find a subject for 'gesacan.' Some say 'he'; others supply 'each,' *i.e., every soul-bearer ... must gain the inevitable place.* The genitives in this case are partitive.—If 'he' be subj., the genitives are dependent on 'gearwe' (= prepared).—The 'he' itself is disputed, some referring it to Grendel; but B. takes it as involved in the parenthesis.

```
            shall slumber
       When feasting is finished. Full was
            the time then
       That the son of Healfdene went to
            the building;
       The excellent atheling would eat of
            the banquet.
20     Ne'er heard I that people with hero-
            band larger
       Bare them better tow'rds their
            bracelet-bestower.
       The laden-with-glory stooped to the
            bench then
       (Their kinsmen-companions in
            plenty were joyful,
       Many a cupful quaffing
            complaisantly),
25     Doughty of spirit in the high-
            tow'ring palace,
       Hrothgar and Hrothulf. Heorot then
            inside
       Was filled with friendly ones;
            falsehood and treachery
       The Folk-Scyldings now nowise did
            practise.
       Then the offspring of Healfdene
            offered to Beowulf
30     A golden standard, as reward for the
            victory,
       A banner embossed, burnie and
            helmet;
       Many men saw then a song-famous
            weapon
       Borne 'fore the hero. Beowulf drank
            of
       The cup in the building; that
            treasure-bestowing
35     He needed not blush for in battle-
            men's presence.
       Ne'er heard I that many men on the
            ale-bench
       In friendlier fashion to their fellows
            presented
       Four bright jewels with gold-work
            embellished.
```

Hrothgar's nephew, Hrothulf, is present. Hrothgar lavishes gifts upon Beowulf.

Four handsomer gifts were never presented.

'Round the roof of the helmet a
   head-guarder outside

40   Braided with wires, with bosses was
   furnished,

That swords-for-the-battle fight-
   hardened might fail

Boldly to harm him, when the hero
   proceeded

Forth against foemen. The defender
   of earls then

Commanded that eight steeds with
   bridles

45   Gold-plated, gleaming, be guided to
   hallward,

Inside the building; on one of them
   stood then

An art-broidered saddle embellished
   with jewels;

'Twas the sovereign's seat, when
   the son of King Healfdene

Was pleased to take part in the play
   of the edges;

50   The famous one's valor ne'er failed
   at the front when

Slain ones were bowing. And to
   Beowulf granted

The prince of the Ingwins, power
   over both,

O'er war-steeds and weapons; bade
   him well to enjoy them.

In so manly a manner the mighty-
   famed chieftain,

55   Hoard-ward of heroes, with horses
   and jewels

War-storms requited, that none e'er
   condemneth

Who willeth to tell truth with full
   justice.

Hrothgar commands that eight finely caparisoned steeds be brought to Beowulf.

XVII.
Banquet (*continued*) - The Scop's Song of Finn and Hnæf

And the atheling of earlmen to
    each of the heroes
Who the ways of the waters went
    with Beowulf,
A costly gift-token gave on the
    mead-bench,
Offered an heirloom, and ordered
    that that man
5   With gold should be paid for,
    whom Grendel had erstwhile
Wickedly slaughtered, as he more
    of them had done
Had far-seeing God and the mood
    of the hero
The fate not averted: the Father
    then governed
All of the earth-dwellers, as He
    ever is doing;
10   Hence insight for all men is
    everywhere fittest,
Forethought of spirit! much he
    shall suffer
Of lief and of loathsome who long
    in this present
Useth the world in this woful
    existence.
There was music and merriment
    mingling together
15   Touching Healfdene's leader; the
    joy-wood was fingered,
Measures recited, when the singer
    of Hrothgar
On mead-bench should mention the
    merry hall-joyance
Of the kinsmen of Finn, when
    onset surprised them:
"The Half-Danish hero, Hnæf of
    the Scyldings,
20   On the field of the Frisians was

Each of Beowulf's companions receives a costly gift. The warrior killed by Grendel is to be paid for in gold.

Hrothgar's scop recalls events in the reign of his lord's father. Hnæf, the Danish general, is treacherously attacked while staying at Finn's castle.

Queen Hildeburg is not only wife of

fated to perish.
Sure Hildeburg needed not mention approving
    The faith of the Jutemen: though blameless entirely,
When shields were shivered she was shorn of her darlings,
Of bairns and brothers: they bent to their fate
25   With war-spear wounded; woe was that woman.
Not causeless lamented the daughter of Hoce
The decree of the Wielder when morning-light came and
She was able 'neath heaven to behold the destruction
Of brothers and bairns, where the brightest of earth-joys
30   She had hitherto had: all the henchmen of Finn
War had offtaken, save a handful remaining,
That he nowise was able to offer resistance[48]
To the onset of Hengest in the parley of battle,
Nor the wretched remnant to rescue in war from
35   The earl of the atheling; but they offered conditions,
Another great building to fully make ready,
A hall and a high-seat, that half they might rule with
The sons of the Jutemen, and that Folcwalda's son would
Day after day the Danemen honor
40   When gifts were giving, and grant of his ring-store
To Hengest's earl-troop ever so

Marginal notes:

Finn, but a kinswoman of the murdered Hnæf.

Finn's force is almost exterminated.

Hengest succeeds Hnæf as Danish general.

Compact between the Frisians and the Danes.

Equality of gifts agreed on.

---

[48] For 1084, R. suggests 'wiht Hengeste wið gefeohtan.'—K. suggests 'wið Hengeste wiht gefeohtan.' Neither emendation would make any essential change in the translation.

freely,
Of his gold-plated jewels, as he
    encouraged the Frisians
On the bench of the beer-hall. On
    both sides they swore then
A fast-binding compact; Finn unto
    Hengest
45   With no thought of revoking
    vowed then most solemnly
The woe-begone remnant well to
    take charge of,
His Witan advising; the agreement
    should no one
By words or works weaken and
    shatter,
By artifice ever injure its value,
50   Though reaved of their ruler their   *No one shall refer to*
    ring-giver's slayer   *old grudges.*
They followed as vassals, Fate so
    requiring:
Then if one of the Frisians the
    quarrel should speak of
In tones that were taunting, terrible
    edges
Should cut in requital.
    Accomplished the oath was,
55   And treasure of gold from the   *Danish warriors are*
    hoard was uplifted.   *burned on a funeral-*
The best of the Scylding braves   *pyre.*
    was then fully
Prepared for the pile; at the pyre
    was seen clearly
The blood-gory burnie, the boar
    with his gilding,
The iron-hard swine, athelings
    many
60   Fatally wounded; no few had been   *Queen Hildeburg*
    slaughtered.   *has her son burnt*
Hildeburg bade then, at the burning   *along with Hnæf.*
    of Hnæf,
The bairn of her bosom to bear to
    the fire,
That his body be burned and borne
    to the pyre.
The woe-stricken woman wept on

his shoulder,[49]

65 In measures lamented; upmounted
    the hero.[50]
The greatest of dead-fires curled to
    the welkin,
On the hill's-front crackled; heads
    were a-melting,
Wound-doors bursting, while the
    blood was a-coursing
From body-bite fierce. The fire
    devoured them,
70 Greediest of spirits, whom war had
    offcarried
From both of the peoples; their
    bravest were fallen.

---

[49] The separation of adjective and noun by a phrase (cf. v. 1118) being very unusual, some scholars have put 'earme on eaxle' with the foregoing lines, inserting a semicolon after 'eaxle.' In this case 'on eaxe' (*i.e.*, on the ashes, cinders) is sometimes read, and this affords a parallel to 'on bæl.' Let us hope that a satisfactory rendering shall yet be reached without resorting to any tampering with the text, such as Lichtenheld proposed: 'earme ides on eaxle gnornode.'

[50] For 'gúð-rinc,' 'gúð-réc,' *battle-smoke*, has been suggested.

XVIII.
The Finn Episode (*continued*) - The Banquet Continues

"Then the warriors departed to go to their dwellings,

Reaved of their friends, Friesland to visit,

Their homes and high-city. Hengest continued

Biding with Finn the blood-tainted winter,

5   Wholly unsundered;[51] of fatherland thought he

Though unable to drive the ring-stemmèd vessel

O'er the ways of the waters; the wave-deeps were tossing,

Fought with the wind; winter in ice-bonds

Closed up the currents, till there came to the dwelling

10   A year in its course, as yet it revolveth,

If season propitious one alway regardeth,

World-cheering weathers. Then winter was gone,

Earth's bosom was lovely; the exile would get him,

The guest from the palace; on grewsomest vengeance

15   He brooded more eager than on

The survivors go to Friesland, the home of Finn. Hengest remains there all winter, unable to get away.

He devises schemes of vengeance.

---

[51] For 1130 (1) R. and Gr. suggest 'elne unflitme' as 1098 (1) reads. The latter verse is undisputed; and, for the former, 'elne' would be as possible as 'ealles,' and 'unflitme' is well supported. Accepting 'elne unflitme' for both, I would suggest '*very peaceably*' for both places: (1) *Finn to Hengest very peaceably vowed with oaths*, etc. (2) *Hengest then still the slaughter-stained winter remained there with Finn very peaceably*. The two passages become thus correlatives, the second a sequel of the first. 'Elne,' in the sense of very (swíðe), needs no argument; and 'unflitme' (from 'flítan') can, it seems to me, be more plausibly rendered 'peaceful,' 'peaceable,' than 'contestable,' or 'conquerable.'

oversea journeys,
Whe'r onset-of-anger he were able
    to 'complish,
The bairns of the Jutemen therein to
    remember.
Nowise refused he the duties of
    liegeman
When Hun of the Frisians the battle-
    sword Láfing,
20   Fairest of falchions, friendly did
    give him:
Its edges were famous in folk-talk
    of Jutland.
And savage sword-fury seized in its
    clutches
Bold-mooded Finn where he bode
    in his palace,
When the grewsome grapple
    Guthlaf and Oslaf
25   Had mournfully mentioned, the
    mere-journey over,
For sorrows half-blamed him; the
    flickering spirit
Could not bide in his bosom. Then
    the building was covered[52]
With corpses of foemen, and Finn
    too was slaughtered,
The king with his comrades, and the
    queen made a prisoner.
30   The troops of the Scyldings bore to
    their vessels
All that the land-king had in his
    palace,
Such trinkets and treasures they
    took as, on searching,
At Finn's they could find. They
    ferried to Daneland
The excellent woman on oversea
    journey,

Guthlaf and Oslaf revenge Hnæf's slaughter.

Finn is slain. The jewels of Finn, and his queen are carried away by the Danes.

The lay is concluded, and the main story is resumed.

---

[52] Some scholars have proposed 'roden'; the line would then read: *Then the building was reddened, etc.,* instead of 'covered.' The 'h' may have been carried over from the three alliterating 'h's.'

35 Led her to their land-folk." The lay
    was concluded,
The gleeman's recital. Shouts again
    rose then,
Bench-glee resounded, bearers then
    offered
Wine from wonder-vats. Wealhtheo
    advanced then
Going 'neath gold-crown, where the
    good ones were seated
40 Uncle and nephew; their peace was
    yet mutual,
True each to the other. And Unferth
    the spokesman
Sat at the feet of the lord of the
    Scyldings:
Each trusted his spirit that his mood
    was courageous,
Though at fight he had failed in
    faith to his kinsmen.
45 Said the queen of the Scyldings:
    "My lord and protector,
Treasure-bestower, take thou this
    beaker;
Joyance attend thee, gold-friend of
    heroes,
And greet thou the Geatmen with
    gracious responses!
So ought one to do. Be kind to the
    Geatmen,
50 In gifts not niggardly; anear and
    afar now
Peace thou enjoyest. Report hath
    informed me
Thou'lt have for a bairn the battle-
    brave hero.
Now is Heorot cleansèd, ring-palace
    gleaming;
Give while thou mayest many
    rewards,
55 And bequeath to thy kinsmen
    kingdom and people,
On wending thy way to the
    Wielder's splendor.
I know good Hrothulf, that the

Skinkers carry round the beaker. Queen Wealhtheow greets Hrothgar, as he sits beside Hrothulf, his nephew.

Be generous to the Geats.

Have as much joy as possible in thy hall, once more purified.

I know that Hrothulf will prove faithful if he survive thee.

noble young troopers
He'll care for and honor, lord of the
    Scyldings,
If earth-joys thou endest earlier than
    he doth;
60   I reckon that recompense he'll
    render with kindness
Our offspring and issue, if that all
    he remember,
What favors of yore, when he yet
    was an infant,
We awarded to him for his worship
    and pleasure."
Then she turned by the bench where
    her sons were carousing,
65   Hrethric and Hrothmund, and the
    heroes' offspring,
The war-youth together; there the
    good one was sitting
'Twixt the brothers twain, Beowulf
    Geatman.

Beowulf is sitting by the two royal sons.

XIX.
Beowulf Receives Further Honor

<table>
<tr><td></td><td>A beaker was borne him, and
    bidding to quaff it</td><td>More gifts are
offered Beowulf.</td></tr>
<tr><td></td><td>Graciously given, and gold that
    was twisted</td><td></td></tr>
<tr><td></td><td>Pleasantly proffered, a pair of arm-
    jewels,</td><td></td></tr>
<tr><td></td><td>Rings and corslet, of collars the
    greatest</td><td></td></tr>
<tr><td>5</td><td>I've heard of 'neath heaven. Of
    heroes not any</td><td>A famous necklace
is referred to, in
comparison with the
gems presented to
Beowulf.</td></tr>
<tr><td></td><td>More splendid from jewels have I
    heard 'neath the welkin,</td><td></td></tr>
<tr><td></td><td>Since Hama off bore the
    Brosingmen's necklace,</td><td></td></tr>
<tr><td></td><td>The bracteates and jewels, from
    the bright-shining city,[53]</td><td></td></tr>
<tr><td></td><td>Eormenric's cunning craftiness
    fled from,</td><td></td></tr>
<tr><td>10</td><td>Chose gain everlasting. Geatish
    Higelac,</td><td></td></tr>
<tr><td></td><td>Grandson of Swerting, last had this
    jewel</td><td></td></tr>
<tr><td></td><td>When tramping 'neath banner the
    treasure he guarded,</td><td></td></tr>
<tr><td></td><td>The field-spoil defended; Fate
    offcarried him</td><td></td></tr>
<tr><td></td><td>When for deeds of daring he
    endured tribulation,</td><td></td></tr>
<tr><td>15</td><td>Hate from the Frisians; the
    ornaments bare he</td><td></td></tr>
<tr><td></td><td>O'er the cup of the currents, costly
    gem-treasures,</td><td></td></tr>
<tr><td></td><td>Mighty folk-leader, he fell 'neath
    his target;</td><td></td></tr>
</table>

---

[53] C. suggests a semicolon after 'city,' with 'he' as supplied subject of 'fled' and 'chose.'

The[54] corpse of the king then came
    into charge of
The race of the Frankmen, the
    mail-shirt and collar:
20   Warmen less noble plundered the
        fallen,
When the fight was finished; the
    folk of the Geatmen
The field of the dead held in
    possession.
The choicest of mead-halls with
    cheering resounded.
Wealhtheo discoursed, the war-
    troop addressed she:
25   "This collar enjoy thou, Beowulf
        worthy,
Young man, in safety, and use thou
    this armor,
Gems of the people, and prosper
    thou fully,
Show thyself sturdy and be to
    these liegemen
Mild with instruction! I'll mind thy
    requital.
30   Thou hast brought it to pass that
        far and near
Forever and ever earthmen shall
    honor thee,
Even so widely as ocean
    surroundeth
The blustering bluffs. Be, while
    thou livest,
A wealth-blessèd atheling. I wish
    thee most truly
35   Jewels and treasure. Be kind to my
        son, thou
Living in joyance! Here each of
    the nobles
Is true unto other, gentle in spirit,
Loyal to leader. The liegemen are

Queen Wealhtheow magnifies Beowulf's achievements.

May gifts never fail thee.

---

[54] For 'feorh' S. suggests 'feoh': 'corpse' in the translation would then be changed to '*possessions*,' '*belongings*.' This is a better reading than one joining, in such intimate syntactical relations, things so unlike as 'corpse' and 'jewels.'

  peaceful,
The war-troops ready: well-
  drunken heroes,[55]
40 Do as I bid ye." Then she went to
  the settle.

    They little know of
    the sorrow in store
    for them.

There was choicest of banquets,
  wine drank the heroes:
Weird they knew not, destiny
  cruel,
As to many an earlman early it
  happened,
When evening had come and
  Hrothgar had parted
45 Off to his manor, the mighty to
  slumber.

    A doomed thane is
    there with them.

Warriors unnumbered warded the
  building
As erst they did often: the ale-
  settle bared they,
'Twas covered all over with beds
  and pillows.
Doomed unto death, down to his
  slumber
50 Bowed then a beer-thane. Their
  battle-shields placed they,

    They were always
    ready for battle.

Bright-shining targets, up by their
  heads then;
O'er the atheling on ale-bench
  'twas easy to see there
Battle-high helmet, burnie of ring-
  mail,
And mighty war-spear. 'Twas the
  wont of that people
55 To constantly keep them equipped

---

[55] S. suggests *'wine-joyous heroes,'* *'warriors elated with wine.'*

for the battle,[56]
At home or marching—in either
    condition—
At seasons just such as necessity
    ordered
As best for their ruler; that people
    was worthy.

---

[56] I believe this translation brings out the meaning of the poet, without departing seriously from the H.-So. text. 'Oft' frequently means 'constantly,' 'continually,' not always 'often.'—Why 'an (on) wíg gearwe' should be written 'ánwíg-gearwe' (= ready for single combat), I cannot see. 'Gearwe' occurs quite frequently with 'on'; cf. B. 1110 (*ready for the pyre*), El. 222 (*ready for the glad journey*). Moreover, what has the idea of single combat to do with B. 1247 ff.? The poet is giving an inventory of the arms and armor which they lay aside on retiring, and he closes his narration by saying that they were *always prepared for battle both at home and on the march.*

XX.
The Mother of Grendel

They sank then to slumber. With
    sorrow one paid for
His evening repose, as often betid
    them
While Grendel was holding[57] the
    gold-bedecked palace,
Ill-deeds performing, till his end
    overtook him,
5   Death for his sins. 'Twas seen very
    clearly,
Known unto earth-folk, that still an
    avenger
Outlived the loathed one, long since
    the sorrow
Caused by the struggle; the mother
    of Grendel,
Devil-shaped woman, her woe ever
    minded,
10   Who was held to inhabit the horrible
    waters,
The cold-flowing currents, after
    Cain had become a
Slayer-with-edges to his one only
    brother,
The son of his sire; he set out then
    banished,
Marked as a murderer, man-joys
    avoiding,
15   Lived in the desert. Thence demons
    unnumbered
Fate-sent awoke; one of them
    Grendel,
Sword-cursèd, hateful, who at
    Heorot met with
A man that was watching, waiting
    the struggle,
Where a horrid one held him with

Grendel's mother is known to be thirsting for revenge.

[Grendel's progenitor, Cain, is again referred to.]

The poet again magnifies Beowulf's valor.

---

[57] Several eminent authorities either read or emend the MS. so as to make
this verse read, *While Grendel was wasting the gold-bedecked palace.*
So 20 15 below: *ravaged the desert.*

> hand-grapple sturdy;
> 20   Nathless he minded the might of his
>   body,
> The glorious gift God had allowed
>   him,
> And folk-ruling Father's favor relied
>   on,
> His help and His comfort: so he
>   conquered the foeman,
> The hell-spirit humbled: he unhappy
>   departed then,
> 25   Reaved of his joyance, journeying to
>   death-haunts,
> Foeman of man. His mother
>   moreover
> Eager and gloomy was anxious to go
>   on
> Her mournful mission, mindful of
>   vengeance
> For the death of her son. She came
>   then to Heorot
> 30   Where the Armor-Dane earlmen all
>   through the building
> Were lying in slumber. Soon there
>   became then
> Return[58] to the nobles, when the
>   mother of Grendel
> Entered the folk-hall; the fear was
>   less grievous
> By even so much as the vigor of
>   maidens,
> 35   War-strength of women, by warrior
>   is reckoned,
> When well-carved weapon, worked
>   with the hammer,
> Blade very bloody, brave with its
>   edges,
> Strikes down the boar-sign that
>   stands on the helmet.
> Then the hard-edgèd weapon was

Grendel's mother comes to avenge her son.

---

[58] For 'sóna' (1281), t.B. suggests 'sára,' limiting 'edhwyrft.' Read then: *Return of sorrows to the nobles, etc.* This emendation supplies the syntactical gap after 'edhwyrft.'

heaved in the building,[59]

40   The brand o'er the benches, broad-
        lindens many
    Hand-fast were lifted; for helmet he
        recked not,
    For armor-net broad, whom terror
        laid hold of.
    She went then hastily, outward
        would get her
    Her life for to save, when some one
        did spy her;

She seizes a favorite liegemen of Hrothgar's.

45   Soon she had grappled one of the
        athelings
    Fast and firmly, when fenward she
        hied her;
    That one to Hrothgar was liefest of
        heroes
    In rank of retainer where waters
        encircle,
    A mighty shield-warrior, whom she
        murdered at slumber,
50   A broadly-famed battle-knight.
        Beowulf was absent,
    But another apartment was erstwhile
        devoted
    To the glory-decked Geatman when
        gold was distributed.

Beowulf was asleep in another part of the palace.

    There was hubbub in Heorot. The
        hand that was famous
    She grasped in its gore;[60] grief was
        renewed then
55   In homes and houses: 'twas no
        happy arrangement
    In both of the quarters to barter and

Beowulf is sent for.

---

[59] Some authorities follow Grein's lexicon in treating 'heard ecg' as an adj. limiting 'sweord': H.-So. renders it as a subst. (So v. 1491.) The sense of the translation would be the same.

[60] B. suggests 'under hróf genam' (v. 1303). This emendation, as well as an emendation with (?) to v. 739, he offers, because 'under' baffles him in both passages. All we need is to take 'under' in its secondary meaning of 'in,' which, though not given by Grein, occurs in the literature. Cf. Chron. 876 (March's A.-S. Gram. § 355) and Oro. Amaz. I. 10, where 'under' = *in the midst of*. Cf. modern Eng. 'in such circumstances,' which interchanges in good usage with 'under such circumstances.'

purchase
With lives of their friends. Then the
    well-agèd ruler,
The gray-headed war-thane, was
    woful in spirit,
When his long-trusted liegeman
    lifeless he knew of,
60   His dearest one gone. Quick from a   *He comes at*
    room was   *Hrothgar's*
Beowulf brought, brave and   *summons.*
    triumphant.
As day was dawning in the dusk of
    the morning,
Went then that earlman, champion
    noble,
Came with comrades, where the
    clever one bided
65   Whether God all gracious would   *Beowulf inquires*
    grant him a respite   *how Hrothgar had*
After the woe he had suffered. The   *enjoyed his night's*
    war-worthy hero   *rest.*
With a troop of retainers trod then
    the pavement
(The hall-building groaned), till he
    greeted the wise one,
The earl of the Ingwins;[61] asked if
    the night had
70   Fully refreshed him, as fain he
    would have it.

---

[61] For 'néod-laðu' (1321) C. suggests 'néad-láðum,' and translates: *asked whether the night had been pleasant to him after crushing-hostility.*

XXI.
Hrothgar's Account of the Monsters

Hrothgar rejoined, helm of the
    Scyldings:
"Ask not of joyance! Grief is
    renewed to
The folk of the Danemen. Dead is
    Æschere,
Yrmenlaf's brother, older than he,
5   My true-hearted counsellor, trusty
    adviser,
Shoulder-companion, when fighting
    in battle
Our heads we protected, when
    troopers were clashing,
And heroes were dashing; such an
    earl should be ever,
An erst-worthy atheling, as Æschere
    proved him.
10   The flickering death-spirit became
    in Heorot
His hand-to-hand murderer; I can
    not tell whither
The cruel one turned in the carcass
    exulting,
By cramming discovered.[62] The
    quarrel she wreaked then,
That last night igone Grendel thou
    killedst
15   In grewsomest manner, with grim-
    holding clutches,
Since too long he had lessened my
    liege-troop and wasted
My folk-men so foully. He fell in
    the battle
With forfeit of life, and another has
    followed,
A mighty crime-worker, her
    kinsman avenging,
20   And henceforth hath 'stablished her

*Hrothgar laments
the death of
Æschere, his
shoulder-
companion.*

*He was my ideal
hero.*

*This horrible
creature came to
avenge Grendel's
death.*

I have heard my

---

[62] For 'gefrægnod' (1334), K. and t.B. suggest 'gefægnod,' rendering
'rejoicing in her fill.' This gives a parallel to 'æse wlanc' (1333).

hatred unyielding,[63]
As it well may appear to many a
   liegeman,
Who mourneth in spirit the treasure-
   bestower,
Her heavy heart-sorrow; the hand is
   now lifeless
Which[64] availed you in every wish
   that you cherished.

25   Land-people heard I, liegemen, this
   saying,
Dwellers in halls, they had seen very
   often
A pair of such mighty march-
   striding creatures,
Far-dwelling spirits, holding the
   moorlands:
One of them wore, as well they
   might notice,

30   The image of woman, the other one
   wretched
In guise of a man wandered in exile,
Except he was huger than any of
   earthmen;
Earth-dwelling people entitled him
   Grendel
In days of yore: they know not their
   father,

35   Whe'r ill-going spirits any were
   borne him
Ever before. They guard the wolf-
   coverts,
Lands inaccessible, wind-beaten
   nesses,
Fearfullest fen-deeps, where a flood
   from the mountains
'Neath mists of the nesses
   netherward rattles,

40   The stream under earth: not far is it
   henceward

Side-notes:

vassals speak of these two uncanny monsters who lived in the moors.

The inhabit the most desolate and horrible places.

---

[63] The line 'And … yielding,' B. renders: *And she has performed a deed of blood-vengeance whose effect is far-reaching.*

[64] 'Sé Þe' (1345) is an instance of masc. rel. with fem. antecedent. So v. 1888, where 'sé Þe' refers to 'yldo.'

Measured by mile-lengths that the
 mere-water standeth,
Which forests hang over, with frost-
 whiting covered,[65]
A firm-rooted forest, the floods
 overshadow.
There ever at night one an ill-
 meaning portent

45 A fire-flood may see; 'mong
  children of men

Even the hounded deer will not seek refuge in these uncanny regions.

None liveth so wise that wot of the
 bottom;
Though harassed by hounds the
 heath-stepper seek for,
Fly to the forest, firm-antlered he-
 deer,
Spurred from afar, his spirit he
 yieldeth,

50 His life on the shore, ere in he will
  venture

To thee only can I look for assistance.

To cover his head. Uncanny the
 place is:
Thence upward ascendeth the
 surging of waters,
Wan to the welkin, when the wind is
 stirring
The weathers unpleasing, till the air
 groweth gloomy,

55 And the heavens lower. Now is help
  to be gotten
From thee and thee only! The abode
 thou know'st not,
The dangerous place where thou'rt
 able to meet with
The sin-laden hero: seek if thou
 darest!
For the feud I will fully fee thee
 with money,

60 With old-time treasure, as erstwhile
  I did thee,
With well-twisted jewels, if away
 thou shalt get thee."

---

[65] For 'hrímge' in the H.-So. edition, Gr. and others read 'hrínde' (=hrínende), and translate: *which rustling forests overhang.*

XXII.
Beowulf Seeks Grendel's Mother

Beowulf answered, Ecgtheow's son:
"Grieve not, O wise one! for each it
   is better,
His friend to avenge than with
   vehemence wail him;
Each of us must the end-day abide
   of
5   His earthly existence; who is able
   accomplish
Glory ere death! To battle-thane
   noble
Lifeless lying, 'tis at last most
   fitting.
Arise, O king, quick let us hasten
To look at the footprint of the
   kinsman of Grendel!
10   I promise thee this now: to his place
   he'll escape not,
To embrace of the earth, nor to
   mountainous forest,
Nor to depths of the ocean,
   wherever he wanders.
Practice thou now patient endurance
Of each of thy sorrows, as I hope for
   thee soothly!"
15   Then up sprang the old one, the All-
   Wielder thanked he,
Ruler Almighty, that the man had
   outspoken.
Then for Hrothgar a war-horse was
   decked with a bridle,
Curly-maned courser. The clever
   folk-leader
Stately proceeded: stepped then an
   earl-troop
20   Of linden-wood bearers. Her
   footprints were seen then
Widely in wood-paths, her way o'er
   the bottoms,
Where she faraway fared o'er fen-
   country murky,

Beowulf exhorts the old king to arouse himself for action.

Hrothgar rouses himself. His horse is brought.

They start on the track of the female monster.

Bore away breathless the best of
    retainers
Who pondered with Hrothgar the
    welfare of country.
25   The son of the athelings then went
        o'er the stony,
Declivitous cliffs, the close-covered
    passes,
Narrow passages, paths
    unfrequented,
Nesses abrupt, nicker-haunts many;
One of a few of wise-mooded
    heroes,
30   He onward advanced to view the
        surroundings,
Till he found unawares woods of the
    mountain
O'er hoar-stones hanging, holt-
    wood unjoyful;
The water stood under, welling and
    gory.
'Twas irksome in spirit to all of the
    Danemen,
35   Friends of the Scyldings, to many a
        liegeman
Sad to be suffered, a sorrow unlittle
To each of the earlmen, when to
    Æschere's head they
Came on the cliff. The current was
    seething
With blood and with gore (the
    troopers gazed on it).
40   The horn anon sang the battle-song
        ready.
The troop were all seated; they saw
    'long the water then
Many a serpent, mere-dragons
    wondrous
Trying the waters, nickers a-lying
On the cliffs of the nesses, which at
    noonday full often
45   Go on the sea-deeps their sorrowful
        journey,
Wild-beasts and wormkind; away
    then they hastened

The sight of Æschere's head causes them great sorrow.

The water is filled with serpents and sea-dragons.

One of them is killed by Beowulf.

Hot-mooded, hateful, they heard the
   great clamor,
The war-trumpet winding. One did
   the Geat-prince
Sunder from earth-joys, with arrow
   from bowstring,
50   From his sea-struggle tore him, that
   the trusty war-missile
Pierced to his vitals; he proved in
   the currents
Less doughty at swimming whom
   death had offcarried.
Soon in the waters the wonderful
   swimmer
Was straitened most sorely with
   sword-pointed boar-spears,
55   Pressed in the battle and pulled to
   the cliff-edge;
The liegemen then looked on the
   loath-fashioned stranger.
Beowulf donned then his battle-
   equipments,
Cared little for life; inlaid and most
   ample,
The hand-woven corslet which
   could cover his body,
60   Must the wave-deeps explore, that
   war might be powerless
To harm the great hero, and the
   hating one's grasp might
Not peril his safety; his head was
   protected
By the light-flashing helmet that
   should mix with the bottoms,
Trying the eddies, treasure-
   emblazoned,
65   Encircled with jewels, as in seasons
   long past
The weapon-smith worked it,
   wondrously made it,
With swine-bodies fashioned it, that
   thenceforward no longer
Brand might bite it, and battle-
   sword hurt it.
And that was not least of helpers in

The dead beast is a poor swimmer.

Beowulf prepares for a struggle with the monster.

He has Unferth's sword in his hand.

<pre>
         prowess
70   That Hrothgar's spokesman had lent
          him when straitened;
      And the hilted hand-sword was
          Hrunting entitled,
      Old and most excellent 'mong all of
          the treasures;
      Its blade was of iron, blotted with
          poison,
      Hardened with gore; it failed not in
          battle
75   Any hero under heaven in hand who   Unferth has little
          it brandished,   use for swords.
      Who ventured to take the terrible
          journeys,
      The battle-field sought; not the
          earliest occasion
      That deeds of daring 'twas destined
          to 'complish.
      Ecglaf's kinsman minded not
          soothly,
80   Exulting in strength, what erst he
          had spoken
      Drunken with wine, when the
          weapon he lent to
      A sword-hero bolder; himself did
          not venture
      'Neath the strife of the currents his
          life to endanger,
      To fame-deeds perform; there he
          forfeited glory,
85   Repute for his strength. Not so with
          the other
      When he clad in his corslet had
          equipped him for battle.
</pre>

XXIII.
Beowulf's Fight with Grendel's Mother

Beowulf spake, Ecgtheow's son:
"Recall now, oh, famous kinsman of
    Healfdene,
Prince very prudent, now to part I
    am ready,
Gold-friend of earlmen, what erst we
    agreed on,

Beowulf makes a parting speech to Hrothgar.

5   Should I lay down my life in lending
    thee assistance,
When my earth-joys were over, thou
    wouldst evermore serve me
In stead of a father; my faithful
    thanemen,
My trusty retainers, protect thou and
    care for,
Fall I in battle: and, Hrothgar
    belovèd,

If I fail, act as a kind liegelord to my thanes, and send Higelac the jewels thou hast given me.

10 Send unto Higelac the high-valued
    jewels
Thou to me hast allotted. The lord of
    the Geatmen
May perceive from the gold, the
    Hrethling may see it
When he looks on the jewels, that a
    gem-giver found I
Good over-measure, enjoyed him
    while able.

I should like my king to know how generous a lord I found thee to be.

15 And the ancient heirloom Unferth
    permit thou,
The famed one to have, the heavy-
    sword splendid[66]
The hard-edgèd weapon; with
    Hrunting to aid me,
I shall gain me glory, or grim-death
    shall take me."
The atheling of Geatmen uttered
    these words and

Beowulf is eager for the fray.

---

[66] Kl. emends 'wæl-sweord.' The half-line would then read, '*the battle-sword splendid.*'—For 'heard-ecg' in next half-verse, see note to 20 39 above.

<table>
<tr><td>20</td><td>Heroic did hasten, not any rejoinder
Was willing to wait for; the wave-
    current swallowed
The doughty-in-battle. Then a day's-
    length elapsed ere
He was able to see the sea at its
    bottom.
Early she found then who fifty of
    winters</td><td>He is a whole day reaching the bottom of the sea.</td></tr>
<tr><td>25</td><td>The course of the currents kept in
    her fury,
Grisly and greedy, that the grim
    one's dominion
Some one of men from above was
    exploring.
Forth did she grab them, grappled
    the warrior
With horrible clutches; yet no
    sooner she injured</td><td>Grendel's mother knows that some one has reached her domains.</td></tr>
<tr><td>30</td><td>His body unscathèd: the burnie out-
    guarded,
That she proved but powerless to
    pierce through the armor,
The limb-mail locked, with loath-
    grabbing fingers.
The sea-wolf bare then, when
    bottomward came she,
The ring-prince homeward, that he
    after was powerless</td><td>She grabs him, and bears him to her den.</td></tr>
<tr><td>35</td><td>(He had daring to do it) to deal with
    his weapons,
But many a mere-beast tormented
    him swimming,
Flood-beasts no few with fierce-
    biting tusks did
Break through his burnie, the brave
    one pursued they.
The earl then discovered he was
    down in some cavern</td><td>Sea-monsters bite and strike him.</td></tr>
<tr><td>40</td><td>Where no water whatever anywise
    harmed him,
And the clutch of the current could
    come not anear him,
Since the roofed-hall prevented;
    brightness a-gleaming</td><td>Beowulf attacks the mother of Grendel.</td></tr>
</table>

Fire-light he saw, flashing
    resplendent.
The good one saw then the sea-
    bottom's monster,
45   The mighty mere-woman; he made a   The sword will not
    great onset   bite.
With weapon-of-battle, his hand not
    desisted
From striking, that war-blade struck
    on her head then
A battle-song greedy. The stranger
    perceived then
The sword would not bite, her life
    would not injure,
50   But the falchion failed the folk-
    prince when straitened:
Erst had it often onsets encountered,
Oft cloven the helmet, the fated
    one's armor:
'Twas the first time that ever the
    excellent jewel
Had failed of its fame. Firm-mooded
    after,
55   Not heedless of valor, but mindful of   The hero throws
    glory,   down all weapons,
Was Higelac's kinsman; the hero-   and again trusts to
    chief angry   his hand-grip.
Cast then his carved-sword covered
    with jewels
That it lay on the earth, hard and
    steel-pointed;
He hoped in his strength, his hand-
    grapple sturdy.
60   So any must act whenever he
    thinketh
To gain him in battle glory
    unending,
And is reckless of living. The lord of
    the War-Geats
(He shrank not from battle) seized
    by the shoulder[67]
The mother of Grendel; then mighty

---

[67] Sw., R., and t.B. suggest 'feaxe' for 'eaxle' (1538) and render: *Seized by the hair.*

<table>
<tr><td></td><td>in struggle</td><td></td></tr>
<tr><td>65</td><td>Swung he his enemy, since his anger was kindled,</td><td>Beowulf falls. The monster sits on him with drawn sword.</td></tr>
<tr><td></td><td>That she fell to the floor. With furious grapple</td><td></td></tr>
<tr><td></td><td>She gave him requital[68] early thereafter,</td><td></td></tr>
<tr><td></td><td>And stretched out to grab him; the strongest of warriors</td><td></td></tr>
<tr><td></td><td>Faint-mooded stumbled, till he fell in his traces,</td><td></td></tr>
<tr><td>70</td><td>Foot-going champion. Then she sat on the hall-guest</td><td>His armor saves his life.</td></tr>
<tr><td></td><td>And wielded her war-knife wide-bladed, flashing,</td><td></td></tr>
<tr><td></td><td>For her son would take vengeance, her one only bairn.</td><td></td></tr>
<tr><td></td><td>His breast-armor woven bode on his shoulder;</td><td></td></tr>
<tr><td></td><td>It guarded his life, the entrance defended</td><td></td></tr>
<tr><td>75</td><td>'Gainst sword-point and edges. Ecgtheow's son there</td><td>God arranged for his escape.</td></tr>
<tr><td></td><td>Had fatally journeyed, champion of Geatmen,</td><td></td></tr>
<tr><td></td><td>In the arms of the ocean, had the armor not given,</td><td></td></tr>
<tr><td></td><td>Close-woven corslet, comfort and succor,</td><td></td></tr>
<tr><td></td><td>And had God most holy not awarded the victory,</td><td></td></tr>
<tr><td>80</td><td>All-knowing Lord; easily did heaven's</td><td></td></tr>
<tr><td></td><td>Ruler most righteous arrange it with justice;[69]</td><td></td></tr>
<tr><td></td><td>Uprose he erect ready for battle.</td><td></td></tr>
</table>

---

[68] If 'hand-léan' be accepted (as the MS. has it), the line will read: *She hand-reward gave him early thereafter.*

[69] Sw. and S. change H.-So.'s semicolon (v. 1557) to a comma, and translate: *The Ruler of Heaven arranged it in justice easily, after he arose again.*

XXIV.
Beowulf is Double-Conqueror

Then he saw mid the war-gems a
    weapon of victory,

Beowulf grasps a giant-sword,

An ancient giant-sword, of edges a-
    doughty,
Glory of warriors: of weapons 'twas
    choicest,
Only 'twas larger than any man else
    was
5   Able to bear to the battle-encounter,
The good and splendid work of the
    giants.
He grasped then the sword-hilt,
    knight of the Scyldings,
Bold and battle-grim, brandished his
    ring-sword,
Hopeless of living, hotly he smote
    her,
10   That the fiend-woman's neck firmly
    it grappled,

and fells the female monster.

Broke through her bone-joints, the
    bill fully pierced her
Fate-cursèd body, she fell to the
    ground then:
The hand-sword was bloody, the
    hero exulted.
The brand was brilliant, brightly it
    glimmered,
15   Just as from heaven gemlike shineth
The torch of the firmament. He
    glanced 'long the building,
And turned by the wall then,
    Higelac's vassal
Raging and wrathful raised his
    battle-sword
Strong by the handle. The edge was
    not useless
20   To the hero-in-battle, but he
    speedily wished to
Give Grendel requital for the many
    assaults he
Had worked on the West-Danes not

once, but often,
When he slew in slumber the
    subjects of Hrothgar,
Swallowed down fifteen sleeping
    retainers
25   Of the folk of the Danemen, and
    fully as many
Carried away, a horrible prey.
He gave him requital, grim-raging
    champion,
When he saw on his rest-place
    weary of conflict
Grendel lying, of life-joys bereavèd,
30   As the battle at Heorot erstwhile had
    scathed him;
His body far bounded, a blow when
    he suffered,
Death having seized him, sword-
    smiting heavy,
And he cut off his head then. Early
    this noticed
The clever carles who as comrades
    of Hrothgar
35   Gazed on the sea-deeps, that the
    surging wave-currents
Were mightily mingled, the mere-
    flood was gory:
Of the good one the gray-haired
    together held converse,
The hoary of head, that they hoped
    not to see again
The atheling ever, that exulting in
    victory
40   He'd return there to visit the
    distinguished folk-ruler:
Then many concluded the mere-
    wolf had killed him.[70]

Beowulf sees the body of Grendel, and cuts off his head.

The waters are gory.

Beowulf is given up for dead.

---

[70] 'Þæs monige gewearð' (1599) and 'hafað þæs geworden' (2027).—In a paper published some years ago in one of the Johns Hopkins University circulars, I tried to throw upon these two long-doubtful passages some light derived from a study of like passages in Alfred's prose.—The impersonal verb 'geweorðan,' with an accus. of the person, and a þæt-clause is used several times with the meaning 'agree.' See Orosius (Sweet's ed.) 178₇; 204₃₄; 208₂₈; 210₁₅; 280₂₀. In the two Beowulf

The ninth hour came then. From the
   ness-edge departed
The bold-mooded Scyldings; the
   gold-friend of heroes
Homeward betook him. The
   strangers sat down then
45   Soul-sick, sorrowful, the sea-waves
      regarding:
They wished and yet weened not
   their well-loved friend-lord
To see any more. The sword-blade
   began then,
The blood having touched it,
   contracting and shriveling
With battle-icicles; 'twas a
   wonderful marvel
50   That it melted entirely, likest to ice
      when
The Father unbindeth the bond of
   the frost and
Unwindeth the wave-bands, He who
   wieldeth dominion
Of times and of tides: a truth-firm
   Creator.
Nor took he of jewels more in the
   dwelling,
55   Lord of the Weders, though they lay
      all around him,
Than the head and the handle

The giant-sword melts.

The hero swims back to the realms of day.

---

passages, the þæt-clause is anticipated by 'þæs,' which is clearly a gen.
of the thing agreed on.

The first passage (v. 1599 (b)-1600) I translate literally: *Then many
agreed upon this (namely), that the sea-wolf had killed him.*

The second passage (v. 2025 (b)-2027): *She is promised ...; to this the
friend of the Scyldings has agreed, etc.* By emending 'is' instead of
'wæs' (2025), the tenses will be brought into perfect harmony.

In v 1997 ff. this same idiom occurs, and was noticed in B.'s great article
on Beowulf, which appeared about the time I published my reading of
1599 and 2027. Translate 1997 then: *Wouldst let the South-Danes
themselves decide about their struggle with Grendel.* Here 'Súð-Dene'
is accus. of person, and 'gúðe' is gen. of thing agreed on.

With such collateral support as that afforded by B. (P. and B. XII. 97), I
have no hesitation in departing from H.-So., my usual guide.

The idiom above treated runs through A.-S., Old Saxon, and other
Teutonic languages, and should be noticed in the lexicons.

handsome with jewels;
The brand early melted, burnt was
    the weapon:[71]
So hot was the blood, the strange-
    spirit poisonous
That in it did perish. He early swam
    off then

60   Who had bided in combat the
        carnage of haters,
Went up through the ocean; the
    eddies were cleansèd,
The spacious expanses, when the
    spirit from farland
His life put aside and this short-
    lived existence.
The seamen's defender came
    swimming to land then

65   Doughty of spirit, rejoiced in his
        sea-gift,
The bulky burden which he bore in
    his keeping.
The excellent vassals advanced then
    to meet him,
To God they were grateful, were
    glad in their chieftain,
That to see him safe and sound was
    granted them.

70   From the high-minded hero, then,
        helmet and burnie
Were speedily loosened: the ocean
    was putrid,
The water 'neath welkin weltered
    with gore.
Forth did they fare, then, their
    footsteps retracing,
Merry and mirthful, measured the
    earth-way,

75   The highway familiar: men very
    daring[72]

It takes four men to
carry Grendel's

---

[71] 'Bróden-mæl' is regarded by most scholars as meaning a damaskeened
sword. Translate: *The damaskeened sword burned up.* Cf. 25 16 and note.

[72] 'Cyning-balde' (1635) is the much-disputed reading of K. and Th. To
render this, "*nobly bold,*" "*excellently bold,*" have been suggested. B.
would read 'cyning-holde' (cf. 290), and render: *Men well-disposed*

<table>
<tr><td></td><td>Bare then the head from the sea-
    cliff, burdening
Each of the earlmen, excellent-
    valiant.
Four of them had to carry with labor
The head of Grendel to the high
    towering gold-hall</td><td>head on a spear.</td></tr>
</table>

80   Upstuck on the spear, till fourteen
        most-valiant
    And battle-brave Geatmen came
        there going
    Straight to the palace: the prince of
        the people
    Measured the mead-ways, their
        mood-brave companion.
    The atheling of earlmen entered the
        building,

85   Deed-valiant man, adorned with
        distinction,
    Doughty shield-warrior, to address
        King Hrothgar:
    Then hung by the hair, the head of
        Grendel
    Was borne to the building, where
        beer-thanes were drinking,
    Loth before earlmen and eke 'fore
        the lady:

90   The warriors beheld then a
        wonderful sight.

---

towards the king carried the head, etc. 'Cynebealde,' says t.B., endorsing
Gr.

XXV.
Beowulf Brings His Trophies - Hrothgar's Gratitude

Beowulf spake, offspring of
   Ecgtheow:

                                          Beowulf relates his last exploit.

"Lo! we blithely have brought thee,
   bairn of Healfdene,
Prince of the Scyldings, these
   presents from ocean
Which thine eye looketh on, for an
   emblem of glory.

5   I came off alive from this, narrowly
       'scaping:
In war 'neath the water the work
   with great pains I
Performed, and the fight had been
   finished quite nearly,
Had God not defended me. I failed
   in the battle
Aught to accomplish, aided by
   Hrunting,

10   Though that weapon was worthy,
    but the Wielder of earth-folk

                                          God was fighting with me.

Gave me willingly to see on the
   wall a
Heavy old hand-sword hanging in
   splendor
(He guided most often the lorn and
   the friendless),
That I swung as a weapon. The
   wards of the house then

15   I killed in the conflict (when
    occasion was given me).
Then the battle-sword burned, the
   brand that was lifted,[73]
As the blood-current sprang, hottest
   of war-sweats;
Seizing the hilt, from my foes I
   offbore it;

---

[73] Or rather, perhaps, '*the inlaid, or damaskeened weapon.*' Cf. 24 57 and note.

I avenged as I ought to their acts of
    malignity,
20 The murder of Danemen. I then
    make thee this promise,

Heorot is freed from monsters.

Thou'lt be able in Heorot careless to
    slumber
With thy throng of heroes and the
    thanes of thy people
Every and each, of greater and
    lesser,
And thou needest not fear for them
    from the selfsame direction
25 As thou formerly fearedst, oh, folk-
    lord of Scyldings,

The famous sword is presented to Hrothgar.

End-day for earlmen." To the age-
    hoary man then,
The gray-haired chieftain, the gold-
    fashioned sword-hilt,
Old-work of giants, was thereupon
    given;
Since the fall of the fiends, it fell to
    the keeping
30 Of the wielder of Danemen, the
    wonder-smith's labor,
And the bad-mooded being
    abandoned this world then,
Opponent of God, victim of murder,
And also his mother; it went to the
    keeping
Of the best of the world-kings,
    where waters encircle,
35 Who the scot divided in Scylding
    dominion.

Hrothgar looks closely at the old sword.

Hrothgar discoursed, the hilt he
    regarded,
The ancient heirloom where an old-
    time contention's
Beginning was graven: the gurgling
    currents,
The flood slew thereafter the race of
    the giants,
40 They had proved themselves daring:
    that people was loth to

It had belonged to a race hateful to God.

The Lord everlasting, through lash
    of the billows

The Father gave them final requital.
So in letters of rune on the clasp of
    the handle
Gleaming and golden, 'twas graven
    exactly,
45   Set forth and said, whom that sword
    had been made for,   Hrothgar praises
                                            Beowulf.
Finest of irons, who first it was
    wrought for,
Wreathed at its handle and
    gleaming with serpents.
The wise one then said (silent they
    all were)
Son of old Healfdene: "He may say
    unrefuted
50   Who performs 'mid the folk-men
    fairness and truth
(The hoary old ruler remembers the
    past),
That better by birth is this bairn of
    the nobles!
Thy fame is extended through far-
    away countries,
Good friend Beowulf, o'er all of the
    races,
55   Thou holdest all firmly, hero-like   Heremod's career
    strength with   is again contrasted
Prudence of spirit. I'll prove myself   with Beowulf's.
    grateful
As before we agreed on; thou
    granted for long shalt
Become a great comfort to kinsmen
    and comrades,
A help unto heroes. Heremod
    became not
60   Such to the Scyldings, successors of
    Ecgwela;
He grew not to please them, but
    grievous destruction,
And diresome death-woes to
    Danemen attracted;
He slew in anger his table-
    companions,
Trustworthy counsellors, till he
    turned off lonely

65	From world-joys away, wide- famous ruler:
	Though high-ruling heaven in hero- strength raised him,
	In might exalted him, o'er men of all nations
	Made him supreme, yet a murderous spirit
	Grew in his bosom: he gave then no ring-gems

A wretched failure of a king, to give no jewels to his retainers.

70 To the Danes after custom; endured
    he unjoyful

Hrothgar moralizes.

Standing the straits from strife that
    was raging,
Longsome folk-sorrow. Learn then
    from this,
Lay hold of virtue! Though laden
    with winters,
I have sung thee these measures.
    'Tis a marvel to tell it,
75 How all-ruling God from greatness
    of spirit
Giveth wisdom to children of men,
Manor and earlship: all things He
    ruleth.
He often permitteth the mood-
    thought of man of
The illustrious lineage to lean to
    possessions,
80 Allows him earthly delights at his
    manor,
A high-burg of heroes to hold in his
    keeping,
Maketh portions of earth-folk hear
    him,
And a wide-reaching kingdom so
    that, wisdom failing him,
He himself is unable to reckon its
    boundaries;
85 He liveth in luxury, little debars
    him,
Nor sickness nor age, no treachery-
    sorrow
Becloudeth his spirit, conflict
    nowhere,

No sword-hate, appeareth, but all of
    the world doth
Wend as he wisheth; the worse he
    knoweth not,
90   Till arrant arrogance inward
    pervading,
Waxeth and springeth, when the
    warder is sleeping,
The guard of the soul: with sorrows
    encompassed,
Too sound is his slumber, the slayer
    is near him,
Who with bow and arrow aimeth in
    malice.

XXVI.
Hrothgar Moralizes - Rest After Labor

"Then bruised in his bosom he with
    bitter-toothed missile
Is hurt 'neath his helmet: from
    harmful pollution
He is powerless to shield him by the
    wonderful mandates
Of the loath-cursèd spirit; what too
    long he hath holden
5   Him seemeth too small, savage he
    hoardeth,
Nor boastfully giveth gold-plated
    rings,[74]
The fate of the future flouts and
    forgetteth
Since God had erst given him
    greatness no little,
Wielder of Glory. His end-day anear,
10   It afterward happens that the bodily-
    dwelling
Fleetingly fadeth, falls into ruins;
Another lays hold who doleth the
    ornaments,
The nobleman's jewels, nothing
    lamenting,
Heedeth no terror. Oh, Beowulf dear,
15   Best of the heroes, from bale-strife
    defend thee,
And choose thee the better, counsels
    eternal;
Beware of arrogance, world-famous
    champion!
But a little-while lasts thy life-
    vigor's fulness;
'Twill after hap early, that illness or
    sword-edge
20   Shall part thee from strength, or the
    grasp of the fire,

Marginal glosses:

A wounded spirit.

Be not over proud: life is fleeting, and its strength soon wasteth away.

Hrothgar gives an account of his

---

[74] K. says '*proudly giveth.*'—Gr. says, '*And gives no gold-plated rings, in order to incite the recipient to boastfulness.*'—B. suggests 'gyld' for 'gylp,' and renders: *And gives no beaten rings for reward.*

Or the wave of the current, or clutch   reign.
  of the edges,
Or flight of the war-spear, or age
  with its horrors,
Or thine eyes' bright flashing shall
  fade into darkness:
'Twill happen full early, excellent
  hero,

25 That death shall subdue thee. So the   Sorrow after joy.
  Danes a half-century
I held under heaven, helped them in
  struggles
'Gainst many a race in middle-
  earth's regions,
With ash-wood and edges, that
  enemies none
On earth molested me. Lo! offsetting
  change, now,

30 Came to my manor, grief after
  joyance,
When Grendel became my constant
  visitor,
Inveterate hater: I from that malice
Continually travailed with trouble no
  little.
Thanks be to God that I gained in my
  lifetime,

35 To the Lord everlasting, to look on
  the gory
Head with mine eyes, after long-
  lasting sorrow!
Go to the bench now, battle-adornèd
Joy in the feasting: of jewels in
  common
We'll meet with many when
  morning appeareth."

40 The Geatman was gladsome, ganged
  he immediately
To go to the bench, as the clever one
  bade him.
Then again as before were the
  famous-for-prowess,
Hall-inhabiters, handsomely
  banqueted,
Feasted anew. The night-veil fell

then
45   Dark o'er the warriors. The courtiers
       rose then;
     The gray-haired was anxious to go to
       his slumbers,
     The hoary old Scylding. Hankered
       the Geatman,
     The champion doughty, greatly, to
       rest him:
     An earlman early outward did lead
       him,
50   Fagged from his faring, from far-
       country springing,
     Who for etiquette's sake all of a
       liegeman's
     Needs regarded, such as seamen at
       that time
     Were bounden to feel. The big-
       hearted rested;
     The building uptowered, spacious
       and gilded,
55   The guest within slumbered, till the
       sable-clad raven
     Blithely foreboded the beacon of
       heaven.
     Then the bright-shining sun o'er the
       bottoms came going;[75]
     The warriors hastened, the heads of
       the peoples
     Were ready to go again to their
       peoples,
60   The high-mooded farer would
       faraway thenceward
     Look for his vessel. The valiant one
       bade then,[76]
     Offspring of Ecglaf, off to bear

Beowulf is fagged,
and seeks rest.

The Geats prepare
to leave Dane-land.

Unferth asks
Beowulf to accept
his sword as a gift.
Beowulf thanks
him.

---

[75] If S.'s emendation be accepted, v. 57 will read: *Then came the light, going bright after darkness: the warriors, etc.*

[76] As the passage stands in H.-So., Unferth presents Beowulf with the sword Hrunting, and B. thanks him for the gift. If, however, the suggestions of Grdtvg. and M. be accepted, the passage will read: *Then the brave one (i.e. Beowulf) commanded that Hrunting be borne to the son of Ecglaf (Unferth), bade him take his sword, his dear weapon; he (B.) thanked him (U.) for the loan, etc.*

Hrunting,
To take his weapon, his well-beloved
    iron;
He him thanked for the gift, saying
    good he accounted
65   The war-friend and mighty, nor chid
    he with words then
The blade of the brand: 'twas a
    brave-mooded hero.
When the warriors were ready,
    arrayed in their trappings,
The atheling dear to the Danemen
    advanced then
On to the dais, where the other was
    sitting,
70   Grim-mooded hero, greeted King
    Hrothgar.

XXVII.
Sorrow at Parting

Beowulf spake, Ecgtheow's offspring:
"We men of the water wish to declare now
Fared from far-lands, we're firmly determined
To seek King Higelac. Here have we fitly
5   Been welcomed and feasted, as heart would desire it;
Good was the greeting. If greater affection
I am anywise able ever on earth to
Gain at thy hands, ruler of heroes,
Than yet I have done, I shall quickly be ready
10   For combat and conflict. O'er the course of the waters
Learn I that neighbors alarm thee with terror,
As haters did whilom, I hither will bring thee
For help unto heroes henchmen by thousands.
I know as to Higelac, the lord of the Geatmen,
15   Though young in years, he yet will permit me,
By words and by works, ward of the people,
Fully to furnish thee forces and bear thee
My lance to relieve thee, if liegemen shall fail thee,
And help of my hand-strength; if Hrethric be treating,
20   Bairn of the king, at the court of the Geatmen,
He thereat may find him friends in abundance:
Faraway countries he were better to

Beowulf's
farewell.

I shall be ever
ready to aid thee.

My liegelord will
encourage me in
aiding thee.

seek for
Who trusts in himself." Hrothgar
  discoursed then,
Making rejoinder: "These words thou
  hast uttered
25 All-knowing God hath given thy
  spirit!

O Beowulf, thou art wise beyond thy years.

Ne'er heard I an earlman thus early in
  life
More clever in speaking: thou'rt
  cautious of spirit,
Mighty of muscle, in mouth-answers
  prudent.
I count on the hope that, happen it
  ever
30 That missile shall rob thee of
  Hrethel's descendant,

Should Higelac die, the Geats could find no better successor than thou wouldst make.

Edge-horrid battle, and illness or
  weapon
Deprive thee of prince, of people's
  protector,
And life thou yet holdest, the Sea-
  Geats will never
Find a more fitting folk-lord to choose
  them,
35 Gem-ward of heroes,
  than *thou* mightest prove thee,

Thou hast healed the ancient breach between our races.

If the kingdom of kinsmen thou carest
  to govern.
Thy mood-spirit likes me the longer
  the better,
Beowulf dear: thou hast brought it to
  pass that
To both these peoples peace shall be
  common,
40 To Geat-folk and Danemen, the strife
  be suspended,
The secret assailings they suffered in
  yore-days;
And also that jewels be shared while I
  govern
The wide-stretching kingdom, and
  that many shall visit
Others o'er the ocean with excellent
  gift-gems:

<table>
<tr><td>45</td><td>The ring-adorned bark shall bring o'er the currents</td><td>Parting gifts</td></tr>
<tr><td></td><td>Presents and love-gifts. This people I know</td><td></td></tr>
<tr><td></td><td>Tow'rd foeman and friend firmly established,[77]</td><td></td></tr>
<tr><td></td><td>After ancient etiquette everywise blameless."</td><td></td></tr>
<tr><td></td><td>Then the warden of earlmen gave him still farther,</td><td></td></tr>
<tr><td>50</td><td>Kinsman of Healfdene, a dozen of jewels,</td><td>Hrothgar kisses Beowulf, and weeps.</td></tr>
<tr><td></td><td>Bade him safely seek with the presents</td><td></td></tr>
<tr><td></td><td>His well-beloved people, early returning.</td><td></td></tr>
<tr><td></td><td>Then the noble-born king kissed the distinguished,</td><td></td></tr>
<tr><td></td><td>Dear-lovèd liegeman, the Dane-prince saluted him,</td><td></td></tr>
<tr><td>55</td><td>And claspèd his neck; tears from him fell,</td><td></td></tr>
<tr><td></td><td>From the gray-headed man: he two things expected,</td><td></td></tr>
<tr><td></td><td>Agèd and reverend, but rather the second,</td><td></td></tr>
<tr><td></td><td>[78]That bold in council they'd meet thereafter.</td><td></td></tr>
<tr><td></td><td>The man was so dear that he failed to suppress the</td><td></td></tr>
<tr><td>60</td><td>Emotions that moved him, but in mood-fetters fastened</td><td>The old king is deeply grieved to part with his benefactor.</td></tr>
<tr><td></td><td>The long-famous hero longeth in secret</td><td></td></tr>
<tr><td></td><td>Deep in his spirit for the dear-beloved man</td><td></td></tr>
</table>

---

[77] For 'geworhte,' the crux of this passage, B. proposes 'geþóhte,' rendering: *I know this people with firm thought every way blameless towards foe and friends.*

[78] S. and B. emend so as to negative the verb 'meet.' "Why should Hrothgar weep if he expects to meet Beowulf again?" both these scholars ask. But the weeping is mentioned before the 'expectations': the tears may have been due to many emotions, especially gratitude, struggling for expression.

Though not a blood-kinsman.
    Beowulf thenceward,
Gold-splendid warrior, walked o'er
    the meadows
65   Exulting in treasure: the sea-going
    vessel
Riding at anchor awaited its owner.
As they pressed on their way then, the
    present of Hrothgar
Was frequently referred to: a folk-
    king indeed that
Everyway blameless, till age did
    debar him
70   The joys of his might, which hath
    many oft injured.

Giving liberally is the true proof of kingship.

XXVIII.
The Homeward Journey - The Two Queens

Then the band of very valiant retainers The coast-guard
Came to the current; they were clad all again.
  in armor,
In link-woven burnies. The land-
  warder noticed
The return of the earlmen, as he
  erstwhile had seen them;
5 Nowise with insult he greeted the
  strangers
From the naze of the cliff, but rode on
  to meet them;
Said the bright-armored
  visitors[79] vesselward traveled
Welcome to Weders. The wide-
  bosomed craft then
Lay on the sand, laden with armor,
10 With horses and jewels, the ring- Beowulf gives
  stemmèd sailer: the guard a
The mast uptowered o'er the treasure handsome
  of Hrothgar. sword.
To the boat-ward a gold-bound brand
  he presented,
That he was afterwards honored on the
  ale-bench more highly
As the heirloom's owner. [80] Set he out
  on his vessel,
15 To drive on the deep, Dane-country left
  he.
Along by the mast then a sea-garment
  fluttered,

---

[79] For 'scawan' (1896), 'scaðan' has been proposed. Accepting this, we may render: *Ho said the bright-armored warriors were going to their vessel, welcome, etc.* (Cf. 1804.)

[80] R. suggests, 'Gewát him on naca,' and renders: *The vessel set out, to drive on the sea, the Dane-country left.* 'On' bears the alliteration; cf. 'on hafu' (2524). This has some advantages over the H.-So. reading; viz. (1) It adds nothing to the text; (2) it makes 'naca' the subject, and thus brings the passage into keeping with the context, where the poet has exhausted his vocabulary in detailing the actions of the vessel.—B.'s emendation (cf. P. and B. XII. 97) is violent.

A rope-fastened sail. The sea-boat resounded,
The wind o'er the waters the wave-floater nowise
Kept from its journey; the sea-goer traveled,
20 The foamy-necked floated forth o'er the currents,

The Geats see their own land again. The port-warden is anxiously looking for them.

The well-fashioned vessel o'er the ways of the ocean,
Till they came within sight of the cliffs of the Geatmen,
The well-known headlands. The wave-goer hastened
Driven by breezes, stood on the shore.
25 Prompt at the ocean, the port-ward was ready,
Who long in the past outlooked in the distance,[81]
At water's-edge waiting well-lovèd heroes;
He bound to the bank then the broad-bosomed vessel
Fast in its fetters, lest the force of the waters
30 Should be able to injure the ocean-wood winsome.
Bade he up then take the treasure of princes,
Plate-gold and fretwork; not far was it thence
To go off in search of the giver of jewels:
Hrethel's son Higelac at home there remaineth,[82]
35 Himself with his comrades close to the sea-coast.

Hygd, the noble queen of Higelac, lavish of gifts.

The building was splendid, the king heroic,

---

[81] B. translates: *Who for a long time, ready at the coast, had looked out into the distance eagerly for the dear men.* This changes the syntax of 'léofra manna.'

[82] For 'wunað' (v. 1924) several eminent critics suggest 'wunade' (=remained). This makes the passage much clearer.

Great in his hall, Hygd very young
    was,
Fine-mooded, clever, though few were
    the winters
That the daughter of Hæreth had dwelt
    in the borough;
40   But she nowise was cringing nor
    niggard of presents,
Of ornaments rare, to the race of the
    Geatmen.
Thrytho nursed anger, excellent[83] folk-
    queen,
Hot-burning hatred: no hero whatever
'Mong household companions, her
    husband excepted
45   Dared to adventure to look at the
    woman
With eyes in the daytime;[84] but he
    knew that death-chains
Hand-wreathed were wrought him:
    early thereafter,
When the hand-strife was over, edges
    were ready,
That fierce-raging sword-point had to
    force a decision,
50   Murder-bale show. Such no womanly
    custom
For a lady to practise, though lovely
    her person,
That a weaver-of-peace, on pretence of
    anger
A belovèd liegeman of life should
    deprive.
Soothly this hindered Heming's
    kinsman;
55   Other ale-drinking earlmen asserted
That fearful folk-sorrows fewer she
    wrought them,

Offa's consort, Thrytho, is contrasted with Hygd. She is a terror to all save her husband.

---

[83] Why should such a woman be described as an 'excellent' queen? C. suggests 'frécnu' = dangerous, bold.

[84] For 'an dæges' various readings have been offered. If 'and-éges' be accepted, the sentence will read: *No hero ... dared look upon her, eye to eye.* If 'án-dæges' be adopted, translate: *Dared look upon her the whole day.*

Treacherous doings, since first she was
    given
Adorned with gold to the war-hero
    youthful,
For her origin honored, when Offa's
    great palace
60   O'er the fallow flood by her father's
    instructions
She sought on her journey, where she
    afterwards fully,
Famed for her virtue, her fate on the
    king's-seat
Enjoyed in her lifetime, love did she
    hold with
The ruler of heroes, the best, it is told
    me,
65   Of all of the earthmen that oceans
    encompass,
Of earl-kindreds endless; hence Offa
    was famous
Far and widely, by gifts and by battles,
Spear-valiant hero; the home of his
    fathers
He governed with wisdom, whence
    Eomær did issue
70   For help unto heroes, Heming's
    kinsman,
Grandson of Garmund, great in
    encounters.

XXIX.
Beowulf and Higelac

Then the brave one departed, his
    band along with him,
Seeking the sea-shore, the sea-
    marches treading,
The wide-stretching shores. The
    world-candle glimmered,
The sun from the southward; they
    proceeded then onward,

5   Early arriving where they heard that
    the troop-lord,
Ongentheow's slayer, excellent,
    youthful
Folk-prince and warrior was
    distributing jewels,
Close in his castle. The coming of
    Beowulf
Was announced in a message
    quickly to Higelac,

10   That the folk-troop's defender forth
    to the palace
The linden-companion alive was
    advancing,
Secure from the combat courtward
    a-going.
The building was early inward made
    ready
For the foot-going guests as the
    good one had ordered.

15   He sat by the man then who had
    lived through the struggle,
Kinsman by kinsman, when the king
    of the people
Had in lordly language saluted the
    dear one,
In words that were formal. The
    daughter of Hæreth
Coursed through the building,

Beowulf and his party seek Higelac.

Beowulf sits by his liegelord.

Queen Hygd receives the heroes.

carrying mead-cups:[85]

20   She loved the retainers, tendered the
        beakers
    To the high-minded Geatmen.
        Higelac 'gan then
    Pleasantly plying his companion
        with questions
    In the high-towering palace. A
        curious interest
    Tormented his spirit, what meaning
        to see in

Higelac is greatly interested in Beowulf's adventures.

25   The Sea-Geats' adventures:
        "Beowulf worthy,
    How throve your journeying, when
        thou thoughtest suddenly
    Far o'er the salt-streams to seek an
        encounter,
    A battle at Heorot? Hast bettered for
        Hrothgar,
    The famous folk-leader, his far-
        published sorrows

Give an account of thy adventures, Beowulf dear.

30   Any at all? In agony-billows
    I mused upon torture, distrusted the
        journey
    Of the belovèd liegeman; I long
        time did pray thee
    By no means to seek out the
        murderous spirit,
    To suffer the South-Danes
        themselves to decide on[86]

My suspense has been great.

35   Grappling with Grendel. To God I
        am thankful
    To be suffered to see thee safe from
        thy journey."
    Beowulf answered, bairn of old
        Ecgtheow:
    "'Tis hidden by no means, Higelac
        chieftain,
    From many of men, the meeting so
        famous,

Beowulf narrates his adventures.

---

[85] 'Meodu-scencum' (1981) some would render *'with mead-pourers.'* Translate then: *The daughter of Hæreth went through the building accompanied by mead-pourers.*

[86] See my note to 1599, supra, and B. in P. and B. XII. 97.

40 What mournful moments of me and
      of Grendel
    Were passed in the place where he
      pressing affliction
    On the Victory-Scyldings
      scathefully brought,
    Anguish forever; that all I avengèd,
    So that any under heaven of the
      kinsmen of Grendel

Grendel's kindred have no cause to boast.

45 Needeth not boast of that cry-in-the-
      morning,
    Who longest liveth of the loth-going
      kindred,[87]
    Encompassed by moorland. I came
      in my journey
    To the royal ring-hall, Hrothgar to
      greet there:
    Soon did the famous scion of
      Healfdene,

Hrothgar received me very cordially.

50 When he understood fully the spirit
      that led me,
    Assign me a seat with the son of his
      bosom.
    The troop was in joyance; mead-
      glee greater
    'Neath arch of the ether not ever
      beheld I
    'Mid hall-building holders. The
      highly-famed queen,

The queen also showed up no little honor.

55 Peace-tie of peoples, oft passed
      through the building,
    Cheered the young troopers; she oft
      tendered a hero
    A beautiful ring-band, ere she went
      to her sitting.
    Oft the daughter of Hrothgar in view
      of the courtiers
    To the earls at the end the ale-vessel
      carried,

Hrothgar's lovely daughter.

60 Whom Freaware I heard then hall-
      sitters title,

She is betrothed to Ingeld, in order to

---

[87] For 'fenne,' supplied by Grdtvg., B. suggests 'fácne' (cf. Jul. 350). Accepting this, translate: *Who longest lives of the hated race, steeped in treachery.*

When nail-adorned jewels she gave
    to the heroes:
Gold-bedecked, youthful, to the glad
    son of Froda
Her faith has been plighted; the
    friend of the Scyldings,
The guard of the kingdom, hath
    given his sanction,[88]

65   And counts it a vantage, for a part of
    the quarrels,
A portion of hatred, to pay with the
    woman.
[89]Somewhere not rarely, when the
    ruler has fallen,
The life-taking lance relaxeth its
    fury
For a brief breathing-spell, though
    the bride be charming!

unite the Danes and Heathobards.

---

[88] See note to v. 1599 above.

[89] This is perhaps the least understood sentence in the poem, almost every word being open to dispute. (1) The 'nó' of our text is an emendation, and is rejected by many scholars. (2) 'Seldan' is by some taken as an adv. (= *seldom*), and by others as a noun (= *page, companion*). (3) 'Léod-hryre,' some render '*fall of the people*'; others, '*fall of the prince.*' (4) 'Búgeð,' most scholars regard as the intrans. verb meaning '*bend,*' '*rest*'; but one great scholar has translated it '*shall kill.*' (5) 'Hwær,' Very recently, has been attacked, 'wære' being suggested. (6) As a corollary to the above, the same critic proposes to drop 'oft' out of the text.—t.B. suggests: Oft seldan wære after léodhryre: lýtle hwíle bongár búgeð, þéah séo brýd duge = *often has a treaty been (thus) struck, after a prince had fallen: (but only) a short time is the spear (then) wont to rest, however excellent the bride may be.*

XXX.
Beowulf Narrates His Adventures to Higelac

"It well may discomfit the prince of
    the Heathobards
And each of the thanemen of earls
    that attend him,
When he goes to the building
    escorting the woman,
That a noble-born Daneman the
    knights should be feasting:
5   There gleam on his person the
    leavings of elders
Hard and ring-bright, Heathobards'
    treasure,
While they wielded their arms, till
    they misled to the battle
Their own dear lives and belovèd
    companions.
He saith at the banquet who the
    collar beholdeth,
10   An ancient ash-warrior who
    earlmen's destruction
Clearly recalleth (cruel his spirit),
Sadly beginneth sounding the
    youthful
Thane-champion's spirit through the
    thoughts of his bosom,
War-grief to waken, and this word-
    answer speaketh:
15   'Art thou able, my friend, to know
    when thou seest it
The brand which thy father bare to
    the conflict
In his latest adventure, 'neath visor
    of helmet,
The dearly-loved iron, where
    Danemen did slay him,
And brave-mooded Scyldings, on
    the fall of the heroes,
20   (When vengeance was sleeping) the
    slaughter-place wielded?
E'en now some man of the
    murderer's progeny

*Ingeld is stirred up
to break the truce.*

Exulting in ornaments enters the
    building,
Boasts of his blood-shedding,
    offbeareth the jewel
Which thou shouldst wholly hold in
    possession!'
25   So he urgeth and mindeth on every
    occasion
With woe-bringing words, till
    waxeth the season
When the woman's thane for the
    works of his father,
The bill having bitten, blood-gory
    sleepeth,
Fated to perish; the other one
    thenceward
30   'Scapeth alive, the land knoweth
    thoroughly.[90]
Then the oaths of the earlmen on
    each side are broken,
When rancors unresting are raging
    in Ingeld
And his wife-love waxeth less warm
    after sorrow.
So the Heathobards' favor not
    faithful I reckon,
35   Their part in the treaty not true to the
    Danemen,
Their friendship not fast. I further
    shall tell thee
More about Grendel, that thou fully
    mayst hear,
Ornament-giver, what afterward
    came from
The hand-rush of heroes. When
    heaven's bright jewel
40   O'er earthfields had glided, the
    stranger came raging,
The horrible night-fiend, us for to
    visit,
Where wholly unharmed the hall we

Having made these preliminary statements, I will now tell thee of Grendel, the monster.

Hondscio fell first.

---

[90] For 'lifigende' (2063), a mere conjecture, 'wígende' has been suggested. The line would then read: *Escapeth by fighting, knows the land thoroughly.*

    were guarding.
    To Hondscio happened a hopeless
        contention,
    Death to the doomed one, dead he
        fell foremost,
45   Girded war-champion; to him
        Grendel became then,
    To the vassal distinguished, a tooth-
        weaponed murderer,
    The well-beloved henchman's body
        all swallowed.
    Not the earlier off empty of hand did
    The bloody-toothed murderer,
        mindful of evils,
50   Wish to escape from the gold-
        giver's palace,
    But sturdy of strength he strove to
        outdo me,
    Hand-ready grappled. A glove was
        suspended
    Spacious and wondrous, in art-
        fetters fastened,
    Which was fashioned entirely by
        touch of the craftman
55   From the dragon's skin by the
        devil's devices:
    He down in its depths would do me
        unsadly
    One among many, deed-doer raging,
    Though sinless he saw me; not so
        could it happen
    When I in my anger upright did
        stand.
60   'Tis too long to recount how requital   *I reflected honor*
        I furnished   *upon my people.*
    For every evil to the earlmen's
        destroyer;
    'Twas there, my prince, that I
        proudly distinguished
    Thy land with my labors. He left and
        retreated,
    He lived his life a little while longer:
65   Yet his right-hand guarded his   *King Hrothgar*
        footstep in Heorot,   *lavished gifts upon*
    And sad-mooded thence to the sea-   *me.*

       bottom fell he,
Mournful in mind. For the might-
     rush of battle
The friend of the Scyldings, with
     gold that was plated,
With ornaments many, much
     requited me,
70   When daylight had dawned, and
     down to the banquet
We had sat us together. There was
     chanting and joyance:
The age-stricken Scylding asked
     many questions
And of old-times related; oft light-
     ringing harp-strings,
Joy-telling wood, were touched by
     the brave one;
75   Now he uttered measures, mourning
     and truthful,
Then the large-hearted land-king a
     legend of wonder
Truthfully told us. Now troubled
     with years
The age-hoary warrior afterward
     began to
Mourn for the might that marked
     him in youth-days;
80   His breast within boiled, when
     burdened with winters
Much he remembered. From
     morning till night then
We joyed us therein as etiquette
     suffered,
Till the second night season came
     unto earth-folk.
Then early thereafter, the mother of
     Grendel
85   Was ready for vengeance, wretched
     she journeyed;
Her son had death ravished, the
     wrath of the Geatmen.
The horrible woman avengèd her
     offspring,
And with mighty mainstrength
     murdered a hero.

The old king is sad over the loss of his youthful vigor.

Grendel's mother.

Æschere falls a prey to her vengeance.

There the spirit of Æschere, agèd adviser,
90 Was ready to vanish; nor when morn had lightened
    Were they anywise suffered to consume him with fire,
    Folk of the Danemen, the death-weakened hero,
    Nor the belovèd liegeman to lay on the pyre;
    She the corpse had offcarried in the clutch of the foeman[91]
95 'Neath mountain-brook's flood. To Hrothgar 'twas saddest
    Of pains that ever had preyed on the chieftain;
    By the life of thee the land-prince then me[92]
    Besought very sadly, in sea-currents' eddies
    To display my prowess, to peril my safety,
100 Might-deeds accomplish; much did he promise.
    I found then the famous flood-current's cruel,
    Horrible depth-warder. A while unto us two
    Hand was in common; the currents were seething
    With gore that was clotted, and Grendel's fierce mother's
105 Head I offhacked in the hall at the bottom
    With huge-reaching sword-edge, hardly I wrested
    My life from her clutches; not doomed was I then,

She suffered not his body to be burned, but ate it. (ll. 90)

I sought the creature in her den, and hewed her head off. (ll. 100)

Jewels were freely bestowed upon me. (ll. 105)

---

[91] For 'fæðmum,' Gr.'s conjecture, B. proposes 'færunga.' These three half-verses would then read: *She bore off the corpse of her foe suddenly under the mountain-torrent.*

[92] [3] The phrase 'þíne lýfe' (2132) was long rendered '*with thy (presupposed) permission.*' The verse would read: *The land-prince then sadly besought me, with thy (presupposed) permission, etc.*

But the warden of earlmen afterward gave me
    Jewels in quantity, kinsman of
        Healfdene.

XXXI.
Gift-Giving is Mutual

"So the belovèd land-prince lived in
    decorum;
I had missed no rewards, no meeds of my
    prowess,
But he gave me jewels, regarding my
    wishes,
Healfdene his bairn; I'll bring them to thee,
    then,

5   Atheling of earlmen, offer them gladly.
And still unto thee is all my affection:[93]
But few of my folk-kin find I surviving
But thee, dear Higelac!" Bade he in then to
    carry[94]
The boar-image, banner, battle-high helmet,

10   Iron-gray armor, the excellent weapon,
In song-measures said: "This suit-for-the-
    battle
Hrothgar presented me, bade me expressly,
Wise-mooded atheling, thereafter to tell
    thee[95]
The whole of its history, said King Heregar
    owned it,

15   Dane-prince for long: yet he wished not to
    give then
The mail to his son, though dearly he loved
    him,
Hereward the hardy. Hold all in joyance!"
I heard that there followed hard on the
    jewels
Two braces of stallions of striking

All my gifts I lay at thy feet.

This armor I have belonged of yore to Heregar.

---

[93] This verse B. renders, '*Now serve I again thee alone as my gracious king.*'

[94] For 'eafor' (2153), Kl. suggests 'ealdor.' Translate then: *Bade the prince then to bear in the banner, battle-high helmet, etc.* On the other hand, W. takes 'eaforhéafodsegn' as a compound, meaning 'helmet': *He bade them bear in the helmet, battle-high helm, gray armor, etc.*

[95] The H.-So. rendering (ærest = *history, origin*; 'eft' for 'est'), though liable to objection, is perhaps the best offered. 'That I should very early tell thee of his favor, kindness' sounds well; but 'his' is badly placed to limit 'ést.'—Perhaps, 'eft' with verbs of saying may have the force of Lat. prefix 're,' and the H.-So. reading mean, 'that I should its origin rehearse to thee.'

    resemblance,
20 Dappled and yellow; he granted him usance
    Of horses and treasures. So a kinsman
      should bear him,
    No web of treachery weave for another,
    Nor by cunning craftiness cause the
      destruction
    Of trusty companion. Most precious to
      Higelac,
25 The bold one in battle, was the bairn of his
      sister,
    And each unto other mindful of favors.
    I am told that to Hygd he proffered the
      necklace,
    Wonder-gem rare that Wealhtheow gave
      him,
    The troop-leader's daughter, a trio of horses
30 Slender and saddle-bright; soon did the
      jewel
    Embellish her bosom, when the beer-feast
      was over.
    So Ecgtheow's bairn brave did prove him,
    War-famous man, by deeds that were
      valiant,
    He lived in honor, belovèd companions
35 Slew not carousing; his mood was not cruel,
    But by hand-strength hugest of heroes then
      living
    The brave one retained the bountiful gift
      that
    The Lord had allowed him. Long was he
      wretched,
    So that sons of the Geatmen accounted him
      worthless,
40 And the lord of the liegemen loth was to do
      him
    Mickle of honor, when mead-cups were
      passing;
    They fully believed him idle and sluggish,
    An indolent atheling: to the honor-blest man
      there
    Came requital for the cuts he had suffered.
45 The folk-troop's defender bade fetch to the
      building
    The heirloom of Hrethel, embellished with

Higelac loves his nephew Beowulf.

Beowulf gives Hygd the necklace that Wealhtheow had given him.

Beowulf is famous.

He is requited for the slights suffered in earlier days.

Higelac overwhelms the

<table>
<tr><td>

    gold,
So the brave one enjoined it; there was
   jewel no richer
In the form of a weapon 'mong Geats of
   that era;
In Beowulf's keeping he placed it and gave
   him

50   Seven of thousands, manor and lordship.
Common to both was land 'mong the
   people,
Estate and inherited rights and possessions,
To the second one specially spacious
   dominions,
To the one who was better. It afterward
   happened

55   In days that followed, befell the battle-
   thanes,
After Higelac's death, and when Heardred
   was murdered
With weapons of warfare 'neath well-
   covered targets,
When valiant battlemen in victor-band
   sought him,
War-Scylfing heroes harassed the nephew

60   Of Hereric in battle. To Beowulf's keeping
Turned there in time extensive dominions:
He fittingly ruled them a fifty of winters
(He a man-ruler wise was, manor-ward old)
   till
A certain one 'gan, on gloom-darkening
   nights, a

65   Dragon, to govern, who guarded a treasure,
A high-rising stone-cliff, on heath that was
   grayish:
A path 'neath it lay, unknown unto mortals.
Some one of earthmen entered the
   mountain,
The heathenish hoard laid hold of with
   ardor;

70   *   *   *   *   *   *
       *   *   *   *   *   *
       *   *   *   *   *   *
       *   *   *   *   *   *
       *   *   *   *   *   *

</td><td>

conqueror
with gifts.

After
Heardred's
death,
Beowulf
becomes
king.

He rules the
Geats fifty
years. The
fire-drake.

</td></tr>
</table>

XXXII.
The Hoard and the Dragon

<pre>
*   *   *   *   *   *
</pre>

He sought of himself who sorely did harm
  him,
But, for need very pressing, the servant of
  one of
The sons of the heroes hate-blows evaded,
5   Seeking for shelter and the sin-driven   The hoard.
  warrior
Took refuge within there. He early looked in
  it,

<pre>
*   *   *   *   *   *
*   *   *   *   *   *
*   *   *   *   * when the onset surprised
</pre>
  him,
10   He a gem-vessel saw there: many of suchlike
Ancient ornaments in the earth-cave were
  lying,
As in days of yore some one of men of
Illustrious lineage, as a legacy monstrous,
There had secreted them, careful and
  thoughtful,
15   Dear-valued jewels. Death had offsnatched
  them,
In the days of the past, and the one man
  moreover
Of the flower of the folk who fared there the
  longest,
Was fain to defer it, friend-mourning
  warder,
A little longer to be left in enjoyment
20   Of long-lasting treasure.[96] A barrow all-
  ready
Stood on the plain the stream-currents nigh
  to,
New by the ness-edge, unnethe of
  approaching:
The keeper of rings carried within a

---

[96] For 'long-gestréona,' B. suggests 'láengestréona,' and renders, *Of fleeting treasures.* S. accepts H.'s 'long-gestréona,' but renders, *The treasure long in accumulating.*

[97]Ponderous deal of the treasure of nobles,

25 Of gold that was beaten, briefly he spake
    then:[98]

    "Hold thou, O Earth, now heroes no more
    may,

The earnings of earlmen. Lo! erst in thy
    bosom

Worthy men won them; war-death hath
    ravished,

Perilous life-bale, all my warriors,

30 Liegemen belovèd, who this life have
    forsaken,

Who hall-pleasures saw. No sword-bearer
    have I,

And no one to burnish the gold-plated
    vessel,

The high-valued beaker: my heroes are
    vanished.

The hardy helmet behung with gilding

35 Shall be reaved of its riches: the ring-
    cleansers slumber

Who were charged to have ready visors-for-
    battle,

And the burnie that bided in battle-encounter

O'er breaking of war-shields the bite of the
    edges

Moulds with the hero. The ring-twisted
    armor,

40 Its lord being lifeless, no longer may journey

Hanging by heroes; harp-joy is vanished,

The rapture of glee-wood, no excellent
    falcon

Swoops through the building, no swift-
    footed charger

Grindeth the gravel. A grievous destruction

45 No few of the world-folk widely hath
    scattered!"

So, woful of spirit one after all

Lamented mournfully, moaning in sadness

By day and by night, till death with its

The ring-giver bewails the loss of retainers.

The fire-dragon

---

[97] For 'hard-fyrdne' (2246), B. first suggested 'hard-fyndne,' rendering: *A heap of treasures ... so great that its equal would be hard to find.* The same scholar suggests later 'hord-wynne dæl' = *A deal of treasure-joy.*

[98] Some read 'fec-word' (2247), and render: *Banning words uttered.*

       billows

       Dashed on his spirit. Then the ancient dusk-
         scather

50   Found the great treasure standing all open,

       He who flaming and fiery flies to the
         barrows,

       Naked war-dragon, nightly escapeth

       Encompassed with fire; men under heaven

       Widely beheld him. 'Tis said that he looks
         for[99]

55   The hoard in the earth, where old he is
         guarding

       The heathenish treasure; he'll be nowise the
         better.

       So three-hundred winters the waster of
         peoples

       Held upon earth that excellent hoard-hall,

       Till the forementioned earlman angered him
         bitterly:

The dragon meets his match.

60   The beat-plated beaker he bare to his
         chieftain

       And fullest remission for all his remissness

       Begged of his liegelord. Then the
         hoard[100] was discovered,

       The treasure was taken, his petition was
         granted

       The lorn-mooded liegeman. His lord
         regarded

65   The old-work of earth-folk—'twas the
         earliest occasion.

       When the dragon awoke, the strife was
         renewed there;

       He snuffed 'long the stone then, stout-
         hearted found he

       The footprint of foeman; too far had he gone

       With cunning craftiness close to the head of

70   The fire-spewing dragon. So undoomed he
         may 'scape from

The hero plunders the dragon's den.

---

[99] An earlier reading of H.'s gave the following meaning to this passage: *He is said to inhabit a mound under the earth, where he, etc.* The translation in the text is more authentic.

[100] The repetition of 'hord' in this passage has led some scholars to suggest new readings to avoid the second 'hord.' This, however, is not under the main stress, and, it seems to me, might easily be accepted.

Anguish and exile with ease who possesseth
The favor of Heaven. The hoard-warden
  eagerly
Searched o'er the ground then, would meet
  with the person
That caused him sorrow while in slumber
  reclining:

75 Gleaming and wild he oft went round the
    cavern,
  All of it outward; not any of earthmen
  Was seen in that desert.[101] Yet he joyed in
    the battle,
  Rejoiced in the conflict: oft he turned to the
    barrow,
  Sought for the gem-cup;[102] this he soon
    perceived then

The dragon perceives that some one has disturbed his treasure.

80 That some man or other had discovered the
    gold,
  The famous folk-treasure. Not fain did the
    hoard-ward
  Wait until evening; then the ward of the
    barrow
  Was angry in spirit, the loathèd one wished
    to
  Pay for the dear-valued drink-cup with fire.

85 Then the day was done as the dragon would
    have it,
  He no longer would wait on the wall, but
    departed
  Fire-impelled, flaming. Fearful the start was
  To earls in the land, as it early thereafter
  To their giver-of-gold was grievously ended.

The dragon is infuriated.

---

[101] The reading of H.-So. is well defended in the notes to that volume. B. emends and renders: *Nor was there any man in that desert who rejoiced in conflict, in battle-work.* That is, the hoard-ward could not find any one who had disturbed his slumbers, for no warrior was there, t.B.'s emendation would give substantially the same translation.

[102] 'Sinc-fæt' (2301): this word both here and in v. 2232, t.B. renders 'treasure.'

XXXIII.
Brave Though Aged - Reminiscences

	The stranger began then to vomit forth fire,	The dragon spits fire.

The stranger began then to vomit
   forth fire,

The dragon spits fire.

To burn the great manor; the blaze
   then glimmered
For anguish to earlmen, not anything
   living
Was the hateful air-goer willing to
   leave there.
5   The war of the worm widely was
   noticed,
The feud of the foeman afar and
   anear,
How the enemy injured the earls of
   the Geatmen,
Harried with hatred: back he hied to
   the treasure,
To the well-hidden cavern ere the
   coming of daylight.
10   He had circled with fire the folk of
   those regions,

Beowulf hears of the havoc wrought by the dragon.

With brand and burning; in the
   barrow he trusted,
In the wall and his war-might: the
   weening deceived him.
Then straight was the horror to
   Beowulf published,
Early forsooth, that his own native
   homestead,[103]
15   The best of buildings, was burning
   and melting,

He fears that Heaven is punishing him for some crime.

Gift-seat of Geatmen. 'Twas a grief
   to the spirit
Of the good-mooded hero, the
   greatest of sorrows:
The wise one weened then that
   wielding his kingdom
'Gainst the ancient commandments,
   he had bitterly angered

---

[103] 'Hám' (2326), the suggestion of B. is accepted by t.B. and other scholars.

20 The Lord everlasting: with lorn
    meditations
His bosom welled inward, as was
    nowise his custom.
The fire-spewing dragon fully had
    wasted
The fastness of warriors, the water-
    land outward,
The manor with fire. The folk-ruling
    hero,
25 Prince of the Weders, was planning
    to wreak him.
The warmen's defender bade them to
    make him,
Earlmen's atheling, an excellent war-
    shield
Wholly of iron: fully he knew then
That wood from the forest was
    helpless to aid him,
30 Shield against fire. The long-worthy
    ruler
Must live the last of his limited
    earth-days,
Of life in the world and the worm
    along with him,
Though he long had been holding
    hoard-wealth in plenty.
Then the ring-prince disdained to
    seek with a war-band,
35 With army extensive, the air-going
    ranger;
He felt no fear of the foeman's
    assaults and
He counted for little the might of the
    dragon,
His power and prowess: for
    previously dared he
A heap of hostility, hazarded
    dangers,
40 War-thane, when Hrothgar's palace
    he cleansèd,
Conquering combatant, clutched in
    the battle
The kinsmen of Grendel, of kindred

[Marginal notes:]

He orders an iron shield to be made from him, wood is useless.

He determines to fight alone.

Beowulf's early triumphs referred to

Higelac's death recalled.

detested.[104]

'Twas of hand-fights not least where Higelac was slaughtered,

When the king of the Geatmen with clashings of battle,

45 Friend-lord of folks in Frisian dominions,

Offspring of Hrethrel perished through sword-drink,

With battle-swords beaten; thence Beowulf came then

On self-help relying, swam through the waters;

He bare on his arm, lone-going, thirty

50 Outfits of armor, when the ocean he mounted.

The Hetwars by no means had need to be boastful

Of their fighting afoot, who forward to meet him

Carried their war-shields: not many returned from

The brave-mooded battle-knight back to their homesteads.

55 Ecgtheow's bairn o'er the bight-courses swam then,

Lone-goer lorn to his land-folk returning,

Where Hygd to him tendered treasure and kingdom,

Rings and dominion: her son she not trusted,

To be able to keep the kingdom devised him

60 'Gainst alien races, on the death of King Higelac.

Yet the sad ones succeeded not in persuading the atheling

In any way ever, to act as a suzerain

To Heardred, or promise to govern

Heardred's lack of capacity to rule.

Beowulf's tact and delicacy recalled.

---

[104] For 'láðan cynnes' (2355), t.B. suggests 'láðan cynne,' apposition to 'mægum.' From syntactical and other considerations, this is a most excellent emendation.

the kingdom;
Yet with friendly counsel in the folk
  he sustained him,
65 Gracious, with honor, till he grew to
  be older,
Wielded the Weders. Wide-fleeing
  outlaws,
Ohthere's sons, sought him o'er the
  waters:
They had stirred a revolt 'gainst the
  helm of the Scylfings,
The best of the sea-kings, who in
  Swedish dominions
70 Distributed treasure, distinguished
  folk-leader.
'Twas the end of his earth-days;
  injury fatal[105]
By swing of the sword he received as
  a greeting,
Offspring of Higelac; Ongentheow's
  bairn
Later departed to visit his homestead,
75 When Heardred was dead; let
  Beowulf rule them,
Govern the Geatmen: good was that
  folk-king.

Reference is here made to a visit which Beowulf receives from Eanmund and Eadgils, why they come is not known.

---

[105] Gr. read 'on feorme' (2386), rendering: *He there at the banquet a fatal wound received by blows of the sword.*

XXXIV.
Beowulf Seeks the Dragon - Beowulf's Reminiscences

He planned requital for the folk-
    leader's ruin
In days thereafter, to Eadgils the
    wretched
Becoming an enemy. Ohthere's son
    then
Went with a war-troop o'er the
    wide-stretching currents
5   With warriors and weapons: with
    woe-journeys cold he

Beowulf has been preserved through many perils.

After avenged him, the king's life he
    took.
So he came off uninjured from all of
    his battles,
Perilous fights, offspring of
    Ecgtheow,
From his deeds of daring, till that
    day most momentous
10   When he fate-driven fared to fight
    with the dragon.

With eleven comrades, he seeks the dragon.

With eleven companions the prince
    of the Geatmen
Went lowering with fury to look at
    the fire-drake:
Inquiring he'd found how the feud
    had arisen,
Hate to his heroes; the highly-famed
    gem-vessel
15   Was brought to his keeping through
    the hand of th' informer.

A guide leads the way, but

That in the throng was thirteenth of
    heroes,
That caused the beginning of
    conflict so bitter,
Captive and wretched, must sad-
    mooded thenceward
very reluctantly.
Point out the place: he passed then
    unwillingly

<pre>
20   To the spot where he knew of the
          notable cavern,
     The cave under earth, not far from
          the ocean,
     The anger of eddies, which inward
          was full of
     Jewels and wires: a warden
          uncanny,
     Warrior weaponed, wardered the
          treasure,
25   Old under earth; no easy possession
     For any of earth-folk access to get
          to.
     Then the battle-brave atheling sat on
          the naze-edge,
     While the gold-friend of Geatmen
          gracious saluted
     His fireside-companions: woe was
          his spirit,
30   Death-boding, wav'ring; Weird very   Beowulf's
          near him,   retrospect.
     Who must seize the old hero, his
          soul-treasure look for,
     Dragging aloof his life from his
          body:
     Not flesh-hidden long was the folk-
          leader's spirit.
     Beowulf spake, Ecgtheow's son:
35   "I survived in my youth-days many   Hrethel took me
          a conflict,   when I was seven.
     Hours of onset: that all I remember.
     I was seven-winters old when the
          jewel-prince took me,
     High-lord of heroes, at the hands of
          my father,
     Hrethel the hero-king had me in
          keeping,
40   Gave me treasure and feasting, our   He treated me as a
          kinship remembered;   son.
     Not ever was I *any* less dear to him
     Knight in the boroughs, than the
          bairns of his household,
     Herebald and Hæthcyn and Higelac
          mine.
     To the eldest unjustly by acts of a
</pre>

kinsman

45   Was murder-bed strewn, since him
     Hæthcyn from horn-bow
  His sheltering chieftain shot with an
     arrow,
  Erred in his aim and injured his
     kinsman,
  One brother the other, with blood-
     sprinkled spear:
  'Twas a feeless fight, finished in
     malice,

One of the brothers accidentally kills another. No fee could compound for such a calamity.

50   Sad to his spirit; the folk-prince
     however
  Had to part from existence with
     vengeance untaken.
  So to hoar-headed hero 'tis heavily
     crushing[106]
  To live to see his son as he rideth
  Young on the gallows: then
     measures he chanteth,

[A parallel case is supposed.]

55   A song of sorrow, when his son is
     hanging
  For the raven's delight, and aged
     and hoary
  He is unable to offer any assistance.
  Every morning his offspring's
     departure
  Is constant recalled: he cares not to
     wait for

---

[106] 'Gomelum ceorle' (2445).—H. takes these words as referring to Hrethel; but the translator here departs from his editor by understanding the poet to refer to a hypothetical old man, introduced as an illustration of a father's sorrow.

Hrethrel had certainly never seen a son of his ride on the gallows to feed the crows.

The passage beginning 'swá bið géomorlic' seems to be an effort to reach a full simile, 'as … so.' 'As it is mournful for an old man, etc. … so the defence of the Weders (2463) bore heart-sorrow, etc.' The verses 2451 to 2463½ would be parenthetical, the poet's feelings being so strong as to interrupt the simile. The punctuation of the fourth edition would be better— a comma after 'galgan' (2447). The translation may be indicated as follows: *(Just) as it is sad for an old man to see his son ride young on the gallows when he himself is uttering mournful measures, a sorrowful song, while his son hangs for a comfort to the raven, and he, old and infirm, cannot render him any kelp—(he is constantly reminded, etc., 2451-2463)—so the defence of the Weders, etc.*

60   The birth of an heir in his borough-
        enclosures,
    Since that one through death-pain
        the deeds hath experienced.
    He heart-grieved beholds in the
        house of his son the
    Wine-building wasted, the wind-
        lodging places
    Reaved of their roaring; the riders
        are sleeping,
65   The knights in the grave; there's no
        sound of the harp-wood,
    Joy in the yards, as of yore were
        familiar.

XXXV.
Reminiscences (*continued*) - Beowulf's Last Battle

"He seeks then his chamber, singeth a woe-song
One for the other; all too extensive
Seemed homesteads and plains. So the helm of the Weders
Mindful of Herebald heart-sorrow carried,

5 Stirred with emotion, nowise was able
To wreak his ruin on the ruthless destroyer:
He was unable to follow the warrior with hatred,
With deeds that were direful, though dear he not held him.
Then pressed by the pang this pain occasioned him,

10 He gave up glee, God-light elected;
He left to his sons, as the man that is rich does,
His land and fortress, when from life he departed.
Then was crime and hostility 'twixt Swedes and Geatmen,
O'er wide-stretching water warring was mutual,

15 Burdensome hatred, when Hrethel had perished,
And Ongentheow's offspring were active and valiant,
Wished not to hold to peace oversea, but
Round Hreosna-beorh often accomplished
Cruelest massacre. This my kinsman avengèd,

20 The feud and fury, as 'tis found on inquiry,
Though one of them paid it with

Hrethel grieves for Herebald.

Strife between Swedes and Geats.

Hæthcyn's fall at Ravenswood.

forfeit of life-joys,
With price that was hard: the
  struggle became then
Fatal to Hæthcyn, lord of the
  Geatmen.
Then I heard that at morning one
  brother the other
25 With edges of irons egged on to   *I requited him for*
    murder,   *the jewels he gave*
Where Ongentheow maketh onset   *me.*
  on Eofor:
The helmet crashed, the hoary-
  haired Scylfing
Sword-smitten fell, his hand then
  remembered
Feud-hate sufficient, refused not
  the death-blow.
30 The gems that he gave me, with
    jewel-bright sword I
'Quited in contest, as occasion was
  offered:
Land he allowed me, life-joy at
  homestead,
Manor to live on. Little he needed
From Gepids or Danes or in
  Sweden to look for
35 Trooper less true, with treasure to   *Beowulf refers to*
    buy him;   *his having slain*
'Mong foot-soldiers ever in front I   *Dæghrefn.*
  would hie me,
Alone in the vanguard, and
  evermore gladly
Warfare shall wage, while this
  weapon endureth
That late and early often did serve
  me
40 When I proved before heroes the
    slayer of Dæghrefn,
Knight of the Hugmen: he by no
  means was suffered
To the king of the Frisians to carry
  the jewels,
The breast-decoration; but the
  banner-possessor
Bowed in the battle, brave-mooded

	atheling.	
45	No weapon was slayer, but war- grapple broke then	He boasts of his youthful prowess, and declares himself still fearless.
	The surge of his spirit, his body destroying.	
	Now shall weapon's edge make war for the treasure,	
	And hand and firm-sword." Beowulf spake then,	
	Boast-words uttered—the latest occasion:	
50	"I braved in my youth-days battles unnumbered;	
	Still am I willing the struggle to look for,	
	Fame-deeds perform, folk-warden prudent,	
	If the hateful despoiler forth from his cavern	
	Seeketh me out!" Each of the heroes,	
55	Helm-bearers sturdy, he thereupon greeted	His last salutations.
	Belovèd co-liegemen—his last salutation:	
	"No brand would I bear, no blade for the dragon,	
	Wist I a way my word-boast to 'complish[107]	
	Else with the monster, as with Grendel I did it;	
60	But fire in the battle hot I expect there,	Let Fate decide between us.
	Furious flame-burning: so I fixed on my body	
	Target and war-mail. The ward of the barrow[108]	

---

[107] The clause 2520(2)-2522(1), rendered by 'Wist I … monster,' Gr., followed by S., translates substantially as follows: *If I knew how else I might combat the boastful defiance of the monster.*—The translation turns upon 'wiðgrípan,' a word not understood.

[108] B. emends and translates: *I will not flee the space of a foot from the guard of the barrow, but there shall be to us a fight at the wall, as fate decrees, each one's Creator.*

I'll not flee from a foot-length, the
    foeman uncanny.
At the wall 'twill befall us as Fate
    decreeth,
65   Each one's Creator. I am eager in
    spirit,   *Wait ye here till*
With the wingèd war-hero to away *the battle is over.*
    with all boasting.
Bide on the barrow with burnies
    protected,
Earls in armor, which of *us* two
    may better
Bear his disaster, when the battle is
    over.
70   'Tis no matter of yours, and man
    cannot do it,
But me and me only, to measure
    his strength with
The monster of malice, might-
    deeds to 'complish.
I with prowess shall gain the gold,
    or the battle,
Direful death-woe will drag off
    your ruler!"
75   The mighty champion rose by his
    shield then,
Brave under helmet, in battle-mail
    went he
'Neath steep-rising stone-cliffs, the
    strength he relied on
Of one man alone: no work for a
    coward.
Then he saw by the wall who a
    great many battles
80   Had lived through, most worthy, *The place of strife*
    when foot-troops collided,   *is described.*
Stone-arches standing, stout-
    hearted champion,
Saw a brook from the barrow
    bubbling out thenceward:
The flood of the fountain was
    fuming with war-flame:
Not nigh to the hoard, for season
    the briefest
85   Could he brave, without burning,

the abyss that was yawning,
The drake was so fiery. The prince
    of the Weders
Caused then that words came from
    his bosom,
So fierce was his fury; the firm-
    hearted shouted:
His battle-clear voice came in
    resounding

90   'Neath the gray-colored stone.
    Stirred was his hatred,   Beowulf calls out
The hoard-ward distinguished the   under the stone
    speech of a man;   arches. The
Time was no longer to look out for terrible encounter.
    friendship.
The breath of the monster issued
    forth first,
Vapory war-sweat, out of the
    stone-cave:

95   The earth re-echoed. The earl   Beowulf
    'neath the barrow   brandishes his
Lifted his shield, lord of the   sword,
    Geatmen,
Tow'rd the terrible stranger: the
    ring-twisted creature's
Heart was then ready to seek for a
    struggle.
The excellent battle-king first
    brandished his weapon,

100   The ancient heirloom, of edges   and stands against
    unblunted,[109]   his shield. The
To the death-planners twain was   dragon coils
    terror from other.   himself.
The lord of the troopers intrepidly
    stood then
'Gainst his high-rising shield,
    when the dragon coiled him
Quickly together: in corslet he
    bided.

---

[109] The translation of this passage is based on 'unsláw' (2565), accepted by
H.-So., in lieu of the long-standing 'ungléaw.' The former is taken as an
adj. limiting 'sweord'; the latter as an adj. c. 'gúð-cyning': *The good war-*
king, rash with edges, brandished his sword, his old relic. The latter gives
a more rhetorical Anglo-Saxon (poetical) sentence.

105 He went then in blazes, bended and
    striding,
  Hasting him forward. His life and
    body
  The targe well protected, for time-
    period shorter
  Than wish demanded for the well-
    renowned leader,
  Where he then for the first day was
    forced to be victor,
110 Famous in battle, as Fate had not
    willed it.
  The lord of the Geatmen uplifted
    his hand then,
  Smiting the fire-drake with sword
    that was precious,
  That bright on the bone the blade-
    edge did weaken,
  Bit more feebly than his folk-
    leader needed,
115 Burdened with bale-griefs. Then
    the barrow-protector,
  When the sword-blow had fallen,
    was fierce in his spirit,
  Flinging his fires, flamings of
    battle
  Gleamed then afar: the gold-friend
    of Weders
  Boasted no conquests, his battle-
    sword failed him
120 Naked in conflict, as by no means
    it ought to,
  Long-trusty weapon. 'Twas no
    slight undertaking
  That Ecgtheow's famous offspring
    would leave
  The drake-cavern's bottom; he
    must live in some region
  Other than this, by the will of the
    dragon,
125 As each one of earthmen existence
    must forfeit.
  'Twas early thereafter the excellent
    warriors
  Met with each other. Anew and

The dragon rages. Beowulf's sword fails him.

The combat is renewed. The great hero is reduced to extremities.

afresh
The hoard-ward took heart (gasps
  heaved then his bosom):
Sorrow he suffered encircled with
  fire
130 Who the people erst governed. His
  companions by no means
Were banded about him, bairns of
  the princes,
With valorous spirit, but they sped
  to the forest,
Seeking for safety. The soul-deeps
  of one were
Ruffled by care: kin-love can never
135 Aught in him waver who well doth
  consider.

His comrades flee!
Blood is thicker
than water.

XLIII.
Wiglaf the Trusty - Beowulf is Deserted by Friends and by Sword

The son of Weohstan was Wiglaf entitled,
Shield-warrior precious, prince of the Scylfings,
Ælfhere's kinsman: he saw his dear liegelord
Enduring the heat 'neath helmet and visor.

5 Then he minded the holding that erst he had given him,
The Wægmunding warriors' wealth-blessèd homestead,
Each of the folk-rights his father had wielded;
He was hot for the battle, his hand seized the target,
The yellow-bark shield, he unsheathed his old weapon,

10 Which was known among earthmen as the relic of Eanmund,
Ohthere's offspring, whom, exiled and friendless,
Weohstan did slay with sword-edge in battle,
And carried his kinsman the clear-shining helmet,
The ring-made burnie, the old giant-weapon

15 That Onela gave him, his boon-fellow's armor,
Ready war-trappings: he the feud did not mention,
Though he'd fatally smitten the son of his brother.
Many a half-year held he the treasures,
The bill and the burnie, till his bairn became able,

20 Like his father before him, fame-

Wiglaf remains true—the ideal Teutonic liegeman.

Wiglaf recalls Beowulf's generosity.

This is Wiglaf's first battle as

deeds to 'complish;
Then he gave him 'mong Geatmen a
  goodly array of
Weeds for his warfare; he went from
  life then
Old on his journey. 'Twas the
  earliest time then
That the youthful champion might
  charge in the battle
25 Aiding his liegelord; his spirit was
  dauntless.
Nor did kinsman's bequest quail at
  the battle:
This the dragon discovered on their
  coming together.
Wiglaf uttered many a right-saying,
Said to his fellows, sad was his
  spirit:
30 "I remember the time when, tasting
  the mead-cup,
We promised in the hall the lord of
  us all
Who gave us these ring-treasures,
  that this battle-equipment,
Swords and helmets, we'd certainly
  quite him,
Should need of such aid ever befall
  him:
35 In the war-band he chose us for this
  journey spontaneously,
Stirred us to glory and gave me these
  jewels,
Since he held and esteemed us trust-
  worthy spearmen,
Hardy helm-bearers, though this
  hero-achievement
Our lord intended alone to
  accomplish,
40 Ward of his people, for most of
  achievements,
Doings audacious, he did among
  earth-folk.
The day is now come when the ruler
  of earthmen
Needeth the vigor of valiant heroes:

liegeman of Beowulf.

Wiglaf appeals to the pride of the cowards.

How we have forfeited our liegelord's confidence!

Our lord is in sore need of us.

Let us wend us towards him, the
   war-prince to succor,
45 While the heat yet rageth, horrible
   fire-fight.
God wot in me, 'tis mickle the liefer
The blaze should embrace my body
   and eat it
With my treasure-bestower.
   Meseemeth not proper
To bear our battle-shields back to
   our country,
50 'Less first we are able to fell and
   destroy the
Long-hating foeman, to defend the
   life of
The prince of the Weders. Well do I
   know 'tisn't
Earned by his exploits, he only of
   Geatmen
Sorrow should suffer, sink in the
   battle:
55 Brand and helmet to us both shall be
   common,
[110]Shield-cover, burnie." Through
   the bale-smoke he stalked then,
Went under helmet to the help of his
   chieftain,
Briefly discoursing: "Beowulf dear,
Perform thou all fully, as thou
   formerly saidst,
60 In thy youthful years, that while yet
   thou livedst
Thou wouldst let thine honor not
   ever be lessened.
Thy life thou shalt save, mighty in
   actions,
Atheling undaunted, with all of thy

Marginal glosses:
- I would rather die than go home without my suzerain.
- Surely he does not deserve to die alone.
- Wiglaf reminds Beowulf of his youthful boasts.
- The monster advances on them.

---

[110] The passage '*Brand ... burnie,*' is much disputed. In the first place, some
eminent critics assume a gap of at least two half-verses.—'Úrum' (2660),
being a peculiar form, has been much discussed. 'Byrdu-scrúd' is also a
crux. B. suggests 'býwdu-scrúd' = *splendid vestments*. Nor is 'bám'
accepted by all, 'béon' being suggested. Whatever the individual words,
the passage must mean, "*I intend to share with him my equipments of
defence.*"

vigor;
I'll give thee assistance." The
dragon came raging,
65 Wild-mooded stranger, when these
words had been uttered
('Twas the second occasion),
seeking his enemies,
Men that were hated, with hot-
gleaming fire-waves;
With blaze-billows burned the board
to its edges:
The fight-armor failed then to
furnish assistance
70 To the youthful spear-hero: but the
young-agèd stripling
Quickly advanced 'neath his
kinsman's war-target,
Since his own had been ground in
the grip of the fire.
Then the warrior-king was careful of
glory,
He soundly smote with sword-for-
the-battle,
75 That it stood in the head by
hatred driven;
Nægling was shivered, the old and
iron-made
Brand of Beowulf in battle deceived
him.
'Twas denied him that edges of irons
were able
To help in the battle; the hand was
too mighty
80 [111]Which every weapon, as I heard
on inquiry,
Outstruck in its stroke, when to
struggle he carried
The wonderful war-sword: it waxed
him no better.
Then the people-despoiler—third of
his onsets—

Beowulf strikes at
the dragon.

His sword fails
him.

The dragon
advances on
Beowulf again.

---

[111] B. would render: *Which, as I heard, excelled in stroke every sword that he carried to the strife, even the strongest (sword).* For 'þonne' he reads 'þone,' rel. pr.

Fierce-raging fire-drake, of feud-
    hate was mindful,
85 Charged on the strong one, when
    chance was afforded,
Heated and war-grim, seized on his
    neck
With teeth that were bitter; he
    bloody did wax with
Soul-gore seething; sword-blood in
    waves boiled.

XXXVII.
The Fatal Struggle - Beowulf's Last Moments

	Then I heard that at need of the king of the people	Wiglaf defends Beowulf.
	The upstanding earlman exhibited prowess,	
	Vigor and courage, as suited his nature;	
	[112]He his head did not guard, but the high-minded liegeman's	
5	Hand was consumed, when he succored his kinsman,	Beowulf draws his knife,
	So he struck the strife-bringing strange-comer lower,	
	Earl-thane in armor, that *in* went the weapon	
	Gleaming and plated, that 'gan then the fire[113]	
	Later to lessen. The liegelord himself then	
10	Retained his consciousness, brandished his war-knife,	and cuts the dragon.
	Battle-sharp, bitter, that he bare on his armor:	
	The Weder-lord cut the worm in the middle.	
	They had felled the enemy (life drove out then[114]	

[112] B. renders: *He (W.) did not regard his (the dragon's) head* (since Beowulf had struck it without effect), *but struck the dragon a little lower down.*—One crux is to find out *whose head* is meant; another is to bring out the antithesis between 'head' and 'hand.'

[113] 'Þæt þæt fýr' (2702), S. emends to 'þá þæt fýr' = *when the fire began to grow less intense afterward.* This emendation relieves the passage of a plethora of conjunctive *þæt*'s.

[114] For 'gefyldan' (2707), S. proposes 'gefylde.' The passage would read: *He felled the foe (life drove out strength), and they then both had destroyed him, chieftains related.* This gives Beowulf the credit of having felled the dragon; then they combine to annihilate him.—For 'ellen' (2707), Kl. suggests 'e(a)llne.'—The reading *'life drove out strength'* is very unsatisfactory and very peculiar. I would suggest as follows: Adopt S.'s emendation, remove H.'s parenthesis, read 'ferh-ellen wræc,' and translate: *He felled the foe, drove out his life-strength* (that is, made

Puissant prowess), the pair had
   destroyed him,
15 Land-chiefs related: so a liegeman
   should prove him,   *Beowulf's wound*
A thaneman when needed. To the   *swells and burns.*
   prince 'twas the last of
His era of conquest by his own great
   achievements,
The latest of world-deeds. The
   wound then began
Which the earth-dwelling dragon
   erstwhile had wrought him
20 To burn and to swell. He soon then   *He sits down*
   discovered   *exhausted.*
That bitterest bale-woe in his bosom
   was raging,
Poison within. The atheling
   advanced then,
That along by the wall, he prudent of
   spirit
Might sit on a settle; he saw the
   giant-work,
25 How arches of stone strengthened   *Wiglaf bathes his*
   with pillars   *lord's head.*
The earth-hall eternal inward
   supported.
Then the long-worthy liegeman
   laved with his hand the
Far-famous chieftain, gory from
   sword-edge,
Refreshing the face of his friend-
   lord and ruler,
30 Sated with battle, unbinding his
   helmet.
Beowulf answered, of his injury
   spake he,
His wound that was fatal (he was
   fully aware
He had lived his allotted life-days
   enjoying
The pleasures of earth; then past was
   entirely

---

him *hors de combat), and then they both, etc.*

<table>
<tr><td>35</td><td>His measure of days, death very
    near):</td><td>Beowulf regrets
that he has no
son.</td></tr>
</table>

35 His measure of days, death very
        near):
    "My son I would give now my
        battle-equipments,
    Had any of heirs been after me
        granted,
    Along of my body. This people I
        governed
    Fifty of winters: no king 'mong my
        neighbors

Beowulf regrets that he has no son.

40 Dared to encounter me with
        comrades-in-battle,
    Try me with terror. The time to me
        ordered
    I bided at home, mine own kept
        fitly,
    Sought me no snares, swore me not
        many
    Oaths in injustice. Joy over all this

I can rejoice in a well-spent life.

45 I'm able to have, though ill with my
        death-wounds;
    Hence the Ruler of Earthmen need
        not charge me
    With the killing of kinsmen, when
        cometh my life out
    Forth from my body. Fare thou with
        haste now
    To behold the hoard 'neath the hoar-
        grayish stone,

Bring me the hoard, Wiglaf, that my dying eyes may be refreshed by a sight of it.

50 Well-lovèd Wiglaf, now the worm is
        a-lying,
    Sore-wounded sleepeth, disseized of
        his treasure.
    Go thou in haste that treasures of old
        I,
    Gold-wealth may gaze on, together
        see lying
    The ether-bright jewels, be easier
        able,
55 Having the heap of hoard-gems, to
        yield my
    Life and the land-folk whom long I
        have governed."

XXXVIII.
Wiglaf Plunders the Dragon's Den - Beowulf's Death

Then heard I that Wihstan's son very
    quickly,
These words being uttered, heeded his
    liegelord
Wounded and war-sick, went in his
    armor,
His well-woven ring-mail, 'neath the
    roof of the barrow.

Wiglaf fulfils his lord's behest.

5   Then the trusty retainer treasure-gems
    many
Victorious saw, when the seat he
    came near to,
Gold-treasure sparkling spread on the
    bottom,
Wonder on the wall, and the worm-
    creature's cavern,
The ancient dawn-flier's, vessels a-
    standing,

The dragon's den.

10   Cups of the ancients of cleansers
    bereavèd,
Robbed of their ornaments: there
    were helmets in numbers,
Old and rust-eaten, arm-bracelets
    many,
Artfully woven. Wealth can easily,
Gold on the sea-bottom, turn into
    vanity[115]

15   Each one of earthmen, arm him who
    pleaseth!
And he saw there lying an all-golden
    banner
High o'er the hoard, of hand-wonders

The dragon is not there.

---

[115] The word 'oferhígian' (2767) being vague and little understood, two quite distinct translations of this passage have arisen. One takes 'oferhígian' as meaning 'to exceed,' and, inserting 'hord' after 'gehwone,' renders: *The treasure may easily, the gold in the ground, exceed in value every hoard of man, hide it who will.* The other takes 'oferhígian' as meaning 'to render arrogant,' and, giving the sentence a moralizing tone, renders substantially as in the body of this work. (Cf. 28 13 et seq.)

greatest,
Linkèd with lacets: a light from it
    sparkled,
That the floor of the cavern he was
    able to look on,
20   To examine the jewels. Sight of the
    dragon
Not any was offered, but edge
    offcarried him.
Then I heard that the hero the hoard-
    treasure plundered,
The giant-work ancient reaved in the
    cavern,
Bare on his bosom the beakers and
    platters,
25   As himself would fain have it, and
    took off the standard,
The brightest of beacons;[116] the bill
    had erst injured
(Its edge was of iron), the old-ruler's
    weapon,
Him who long had watched as ward
    of the jewels,
Who fire-terror carried hot for the
    treasure,
30   Rolling in battle, in middlemost
    darkness,
Till murdered he perished. The
    messenger hastened,
Not loth to return, hurried by jewels:
Curiosity urged him if, excellent-
    mooded,
Alive he should find the lord of the
    Weders
35   Mortally wounded, at the place where
    he left him.
'Mid the jewels he found then the
    famous old chieftain,
His liegelord belovèd, at his life's-end

Wiglaf bears the hoard away.

---

[116] The passage beginning here is very much disputed. 'The bill of the old
lord' is by some regarded as Beowulf's sword; by others, as that of the
ancient possessor of the hoard. 'Ær gescód' (2778), translated in this work
as verb and adverb, is by some regarded as a compound participial adj.
= *sheathed in brass.*

gory:
He thereupon 'gan to lave him with
 water,
Till the point of his word piercèd his
 breast-hoard.

40 Beowulf spake (the gold-gems he
 noticed),
The old one in sorrow: "For the
 jewels I look on
Thanks do I utter for all to the Ruler,
Wielder of Worship, with words of
 devotion,
The Lord everlasting, that He let me
 such treasures

45 Gain for my people ere death
 overtook me.
Since I've bartered the agèd life to me
 granted
For treasure of jewels, attend ye
 henceforward
The wants of the war-thanes; I can
 wait here no longer.
The battle-famed bid ye to build them
 a grave-hill,

50 Bright when I'm burned, at the brim-
 current's limit;
As a memory-mark to the men I have
 governed,
Aloft it shall tower on Whale's-Ness
 uprising,
That earls of the ocean hereafter may
 call it
Beowulf's barrow, those who barks
 ever-dashing

55 From a distance shall drive o'er the
 darkness of waters."
The bold-mooded troop-lord took
 from his neck then
The ring that was golden, gave to his
 liegeman,
The youthful war-hero, his gold-
 flashing helmet,
His collar and war-mail, bade him
 well to enjoy them:

60 "Thou art latest left of the line of our

Beowulf is
rejoiced to see the
jewels.

He desires to be
held in memory
by his people.

The hero's last
gift and last
words.

kindred,
Of Wægmunding people: Weird hath
    offcarried
All of my kinsmen to the Creator's
    glory,
Earls in their vigor: I shall after them
    fare."
'Twas the aged liegelord's last-
    spoken word in
65   His musings of spirit, ere he mounted
    the fire,
The battle-waves burning: from his
    bosom departed
His soul to seek the sainted ones'
    glory.

XXXIX.
The Dead Foes - Wiglaf's Bitter Taunts

It had wofully chanced then the
  youthful retainer
To behold on earth the most ardent-
  belovèd
At his life-days' limit, lying there
  helpless.
The slayer too lay there, of life all
  bereavèd,
5 Horrible earth-drake, harassed with
    sorrow:
The round-twisted monster was
  permitted no longer
To govern the ring-hoards, but edges
  of war-swords
Mightily seized him, battle-sharp,
  sturdy
Leavings of hammers, that still from
  his wounds
10 The flier-from-farland fell to the
    earth
Hard by his hoard-house, hopped he
  at midnight
Not e'er through the air, nor exulting
  in jewels
Suffered them to see him: but he sank
  then to earthward
Through the hero-chief's handwork. I
  heard sure it throve then
15 But few in the land of liegemen of
    valor,
Though of every achievement bold he
  had proved him,
To run 'gainst the breath of the
  venomous scather,
Or the hall of the treasure to trouble
  with hand-blows,
If he watching had found the ward of
  the hoard-hall
20 On the barrow abiding. Beowulf's
    part of
The treasure of jewels was paid for

Wiglaf is sorely grieved to see his lord look so un-warlike.

The dragon has plundered his last hoard.

Few warriors dared to face the monster.

The cowardly thanes come out of the thicket.

with death;
Each of the twain had attained to the
   end of
Life so unlasting. Not long was the
   time till
The tardy-at-battle returned from the
   thicket,

25   The timid truce-breakers ten all
     together,   *They are ashamed*
                                  of their desertion.
Who durst not before play with the
   lances
In the prince of the people's pressing
   emergency;
But blushing with shame, with
   shields they betook them,
With arms and armor where the old
   one was lying:

30   They gazed upon Wiglaf. He was
   sitting exhausted,
Foot-going fighter, not far from the
   shoulders
Of the lord of the people, would
   rouse him with water;
No whit did it help him; though he
   hoped for it keenly,
He was able on earth not at all in the
   leader

35   Life to retain, and nowise to alter   *Wiglaf is ready to*
The will of the Wielder; the World-   *excoriate them.*
   Ruler's power[117]
Would govern the actions of each one
   of heroes,
As yet He is doing. From the young
   one forthwith then
Could grim-worded greeting be got
   for him quickly

40   Whose courage had failed him.   *He begins to taunt*
   Wiglaf discoursed then,   *them.*
Weohstan his son, sad-mooded hero,
Looked on the hated: "He who
   soothness will utter

---

[117] For 'dædum rædan' (2859) B. suggests 'déað áraedan,' and renders: *The might (or judgment) of God would determine death for every man, as he still does.*

Can say that the liegelord who gave
    you the jewels,
The ornament-armor wherein ye are
    standing,

45   When on ale-bench often he offered
    to hall-men
Helmet and burnie, the prince to his
    liegemen,
As best upon earth he was able to
    find him,—
That he wildly wasted his war-gear
    undoubtedly
When battle o'ertook him.[118] The
    troop-king no need had

Surely our lord wasted his armor on poltroons.

50   To glory in comrades; yet God
    permitted him,
Victory-Wielder, with weapon
    unaided
Himself to avenge, when vigor was
    needed.
I life-protection but little was able
To give him in battle, and I 'gan,
    notwithstanding,

He, however, got along without you. With some aid, I could have saved our liegelord.

55   Helping my kinsman (my strength
    overtaxing):
He waxed the weaker when with
    weapon I smote on
My mortal opponent, the fire less
    strongly
Flamed from his bosom. Too few of
    protectors
Came round the king at the critical
    moment.

Gift-giving is over with your people: the ring-lord is dead.

60   Now must ornament-taking and
    weapon-bestowing,
Home-joyance all, cease for your
    kindred,
Food for the people; each of your
    warriors
Must needs be bereavèd of rights that
    he holdeth

---

[118] Some critics, H. himself in earlier editions, put the clause, 'When … him' (A.-S. 'þá … beget') with the following sentence; that is, they make it dependent upon 'þorfte' (2875) instead of upon 'forwurpe' (2873).

In landed possessions, when faraway
   nobles
65 Shall learn of your leaving your lord
   so basely,   *What is life
                 without honor?*
The dastardly deed. Death is more
   pleasant
To every earlman than infamous life
   is!"

XL.
The Messenger of Death

Then he charged that the battle be announced at the hedge	Wiglaf sends the news of Beowulf's death to liegemen near by.
Up o'er the cliff-edge, where the earl-troopers bided	
The whole of the morning, mood-wretched sat them,	
Bearers of battle-shields, both things expecting,	
5 The end of his lifetime and the coming again of	The messenger speaks.
The liegelord belovèd. Little reserved he	
Of news that was known, who the ness-cliff did travel,	
But he truly discoursed to all that could hear him:	
"Now the free-giving friend-lord of the folk of the Weders,	
10 The folk-prince of Geatmen, is fast in his death-bed,	Wiglaf sits by our dead lord.
By the deeds of the dragon in death-bed abideth;	
Along with him lieth his life-taking foeman	
Slain with knife-wounds: he was wholly unable	
To injure at all the ill-planning monster	
15 With bite of his sword-edge. Wiglaf is sitting,	Our lord's death will lead to attacks from our old foes.
Offspring of Wihstan, up over Beowulf,	
Earl o'er another whose end-day hath reached him,	
Head-watch holdeth o'er heroes unliving,[119]	

---

[119] 'Hige-méðum' (2910) is glossed by H. as dat. plu. (= for the dead). S. proposes 'hige-méðe,' nom. sing. limiting Wigláf; i.e. *W., mood-weary, holds head-watch o'er friend and foe.*—B. suggests taking the word as dat. inst. plu. of an abstract noun in -'u.' The translation would be

For friend and for foeman. The folk
    now expecteth

20   A season of strife when the death of   Higelac's death
    the folk-king   recalled.

To Frankmen and Frisians in far-
    lands is published.

The war-hatred waxed warm 'gainst
    the Hugmen,

When Higelac came with an army of
    vessels

Faring to Friesland, where the
    Frankmen in battle

25   Humbled him and bravely with
    overmight 'complished

That the mail-clad warrior must sink
    in the battle,

Fell 'mid his folk-troop: no fret-
    gems presented

The atheling to earlmen; aye was
    denied us

Merewing's mercy. The men of the
    Swedelands

30   For truce or for truth trust I but little;   Hæthcyn's fall

But widely 'twas known that near   referred to.
    Ravenswood Ongentheow

Sundered Hæthcyn the Hrethling
    from life-joys,

When for pride overweening the
    War-Scylfings first did

Seek the Geatmen with savage
    intentions.

35   Early did Ohthere's age-laden
    father,

Old and terrible, give blow in
    requital,

Killing the sea-king, the queen-
    mother rescued,

The old one his consort deprived of
    her gold,

Onela's mother and Ohthere's also,

40   And then followed the feud-nursing
    foemen till hardly,

---

substantially the same as S.'s.

Reaved of their ruler, they
    Ravenswood entered.
Then with vast-numbered forces he
    assaulted the remnant,
Weary with wounds, woe often
    promised
The livelong night to the sad-hearted
    war-troop:
45   Said he at morning would kill them
    with edges of weapons,
Some on the gallows for glee to the
    fowls.
Aid came after to the anxious-in-
    spirit
At dawn of the day, after Higelac's
    bugle
And trumpet-sound heard they,
    when the good one proceeded
50   And faring followed the flower of
    the troopers.

XLI.
The Messenger's Retrospect

"The blood-stainèd trace of Swedes
and Geatmen,
The death-rush of warmen, widely
was noticed,
How the folks with each other feud
did awaken.
The worthy one went then[120] with
well-beloved comrades,

5   Old and dejected to go to the
fastness,
Ongentheo earl upward then turned
him;
Of Higelac's battle he'd heard on
inquiry,
The exultant one's prowess,
despaired of resistance,
With earls of the ocean to be able to
struggle,

10   'Gainst sea-going sailors to save the
hoard-treasure,
His wife and his children; he fled
after thenceward
Old 'neath the earth-wall. Then was
offered pursuance
To the braves of the Swedemen, the
banner[121] to Higelac.
They fared then forth o'er the field-
of-protection,

15   When the Hrethling heroes
hedgeward had thronged them.
Then with edges of irons was
Ongentheow driven,

The messenger
continues, and
refers to the feuds
of Swedes and
Geats.

Wulf wounds
Ongentheow.

---

[120] For 'góda,' which seems a surprising epithet for a Geat to apply to the "terrible" Ongentheow, B. suggests 'gomela.' The passage would then stand: '*The old one went then,*' etc.

[121] For 'segn Higeláce,' K., Th., and B. propose 'segn Higeláces,' meaning: *Higelac's banner followed the Swedes (in pursuit).*—S. suggests 'sæcc Higeláces,' and renders: *Higelac's pursuit.*—The H.-So. reading, as translated in our text, means that the banner of the enemy was captured and brought to Higelac as a trophy.

The gray-haired to tarry, that the
   troop-ruler had to
Suffer the power solely of Eofor:
Wulf then wildly with weapon
   assaulted him,
20 Wonred his son, that for swinge of
    the edges
The blood from his body burst out
   in currents,
Forth 'neath his hair. He feared not
   however,
Gray-headed Scylfing, but speedily
   quited
The wasting wound-stroke with
   worse exchange,
25 When the king of the thane-troop
    thither did turn him:
The wise-mooded son of Wonred
   was powerless
To give a return-blow to the age-
   hoary man,
But his head-shielding helmet first
   hewed he to pieces,
That flecked with gore perforce he
   did totter,
30 Fell to the earth; not fey was he yet
    then,
But up did he spring though an
   edge-wound had reached him.
Then Higelac's vassal, valiant and
   dauntless,
When his brother lay dead, made his
   broad-bladed weapon,
Giant-sword ancient, defence of the
   giants,
35 Bound o'er the shield-wall; the folk-
    prince succumbed then,
Shepherd of people, was pierced to
   the vitals.
There were many attendants who
   bound up his kinsman,
Carried him quickly when occasion
   was granted
That the place of the slain they were
   suffered to manage.

Ongentheow gives a stout blow in return.

Eofor smites Ongentheow fiercely.

Ongentheow is slain.

<table>
<tr><td>40</td><td>This pending, one hero plundered the other,
His armor of iron from Ongentheow ravished,
His hard-sword hilted and helmet together;
The old one's equipments he carried to Higelac.
He the jewels received, and rewards 'mid the troopers</td><td>Eofor takes the old king's war-gear to Higelac.</td></tr>
<tr><td>45</td><td>Graciously promised, and so did accomplish:
The king of the Weders requited the war-rush,
Hrethel's descendant, when home he repaired him,
To Eofor and Wulf with wide-lavished treasures,
To each of them granted a hundred of thousands</td><td>Higelac rewards the brothers.</td></tr>
<tr><td>50</td><td>In land and rings wrought out of wire:
None upon mid-earth needed to twit him[122]
With the gifts he gave them, when glory they conquered;
And to Eofor then gave he his one only daughter,
The honor of home, as an earnest of favor.</td><td>His gifts were beyond cavil. To Eofor he also gives his only daughter in marriage.</td></tr>
<tr><td>55</td><td>That's the feud and hatred—as ween I 'twill happen—
The anger of earthmen, that earls of the Swedemen
Will visit on us, when they hear that our leader
Lifeless is lying, he who longtime protected
His hoard and kingdom 'gainst</td><td></td></tr>
</table>

---

[122] The rendering given in this translation represents the king as being generous beyond the possibility of reproach; but some authorities construe 'him' (2996) as plu., and understand the passage to mean that no one reproached the two brothers with having received more reward than they were entitled to.

> hating assailers,
> 60   Who on the fall of the heroes defended of yore
>   The deed-mighty Scyldings,[123] did for the troopers
>   What best did avail them, and further moreover
>   Hero-deeds 'complished. Now is haste most fitting,
>   That the lord of liegemen we look upon yonder,
> 65   And *that* one carry on journey to death-pyre
>   Who ring-presents gave us. Not aught of it all
>   Shall melt with the brave one— there's a mass of bright jewels,
>   Gold beyond measure, grewsomely purchased
>   And ending it all ornament-rings too
> 70   Bought with his life; these fire shall devour,
>   Flame shall cover, no earlman shall wear
>   A jewel-memento, nor beautiful virgin
>   Have on her neck rings to adorn her,
>   But wretched in spirit bereavèd of gold-gems
> 75   She shall oft with others be exiled and banished,
>   Since the leader of liegemen hath laughter forsaken,
>   Mirth and merriment. Hence many a war-spear
>   Cold from the morning shall be clutched in the fingers,

It is time for us to pay the last marks of respect to our lord.

---

[123] The name 'Scyldingas' here (3006) has caused much discussion, and given rise to several theories, the most important of which are as follows: (1) After the downfall of Hrothgar's family, Beowulf was king of the Danes, or Scyldings. (2) For 'Scyldingas' read 'Scylfingas'— that is, after killing Eadgils, the Scylfing prince, Beowulf conquered his land, and held it in subjection. (3) M. considers 3006 a thoughtless repetition of 2053. (Cf. H.-So.)

Heaved in the hand, no harp-
    music's sound shall

80   Waken the warriors, but the wan-
    coated raven

Fain over fey ones freely shall
    gabble,

Shall say to the eagle how he sped
    in the eating,

When, the wolf his companion, he
    plundered the slain."

So the high-minded hero was
    rehearsing these stories

85   Loathsome to hear; he lied as to few
    of

Weirds and of words. All the war-
    troop arose then,

'Neath the Eagle's Cape sadly
    betook them,

Weeping and woful, the wonder to
    look at.

They saw on the sand then soulless
    a-lying,

90   His slaughter-bed holding, him who
    rings had given them

In days that were done; then the
    death-bringing moment

Was come to the good one, that the
    king very warlike,

Wielder of Weders, with wonder-
    death perished.

First they beheld there a creature
    more wondrous,

95   The worm on the field, in front of
    them lying,

The foeman before them: the fire-
    spewing dragon,

Ghostly and grisly guest in his
    terrors,

Was scorched in the fire; as he lay
    there he measured

Fifty of feet; came forth in the
    night-time[124]

> The warriors go sadly to look at Beowulf's lifeless body.

> They also see the dragon.

---

[124] B. takes 'nihtes' and 'hwílum' (3045) as separate adverbial cases, and renders: *Joy in the air had he of yore by night, etc.* He thinks that the idea

100 To rejoice in the air, thereafter
    departing
To visit his den; he in death was
    then fastened,
He would joy in no other earth-
    hollowed caverns.
There stood round about him
    beakers and vessels,
Dishes were lying and dear-valued
    weapons,
105 With iron-rust eaten, as in earth's   The hoard was
    mighty bosom   under a magic spell.
A thousand of winters there they
    had rested:
That mighty bequest then with
    magic was guarded,
Gold of the ancients, that earlman
    not any
The ring-hall could touch, save
    Ruling-God only,
110 Sooth-king of Vict'ries gave whom   God alone could
    He wished to   give access to it.
  [125] (He is earth-folk's protector) to
    open the treasure,
E'en to such among mortals as
    seemed to Him proper.

---

  of vanished time ought to be expressed.

[125] The parenthesis is by some emended so as to read: (1) (*He* (i.e. *God*) *is the hope of men*); (2) (*he is the hope of heroes*). Gr.'s reading has no parenthesis, but says: … *could touch, unless God himself, true king of victories, gave to whom he would to open the treasure, the secret place of enchanters, etc.* The last is rejected on many grounds.

XLII.
Wiglaf's Sad Story The Hoard Carried Off

  Then 'twas seen that the journey
   prospered him little
  Who wrongly within had the
   ornaments hidden[126]
  Down 'neath the wall. The warden
   erst slaughtered
  Some few of the folk-troop: the feud
   then thereafter
5 Was hotly avengèd. 'Tis a wonder
   where,[127]
  When the strength-famous trooper
   has attained to the end of
  Life-days allotted, then no longer the
   man may
  Remain with his kinsmen where
   mead-cups are flowing.
  So to Beowulf happened when the
   ward of the barrow,
10 Assaults, he sought for: himself had
   no knowledge
  How his leaving this life was likely
   to happen.
  So to doomsday, famous folk-leaders
   down did
  Call it with curses—who
   'complished it there—
  That that man should be ever of ill-
   deeds convicted,

---

[126] For 'gehýdde,' B. suggests 'gehýðde': the passage would stand as above except the change of 'hidden' (v. 2) to 'plundered.' The reference, however, would be to the thief, not to the dragon.

[127] The passage 'Wundur ... búan' (3063-3066), M. took to be a question asking whether it was strange that a man should die when his appointed time had come.—B. sees a corruption, and makes emendations introducing the idea that a brave man should not die from sickness or from old age, but should find death in the performance of some deed of daring.—S. sees an indirect question introduced by 'hwár' and dependent upon 'wundur': *A secret is it when the hero is to die, etc.*—Why may the two clauses not be parallel, and the whole passage an Old English cry of *'How wonderful is death!'?*—S.'s is the best yet offered, if 'wundor' means 'mystery.'

<table>
<tr><td>15</td><td>Confined in foul-places, fastened in
    hell-bonds,
Punished with plagues, who this
    place should e'er ravage.[128]
He cared not for gold: rather the
    Wielder's
Favor preferred he first to get sight
    of.[129]
Wiglaf discoursed then, Wihstan his
    son:</td><td>Wiglaf addresses
his comrades.</td></tr>
<tr><td>20</td><td>"Oft many an earlman on one man's
    account must
Sorrow endure, as to us it hath
    happened.
The liegelord belovèd we could little
    prevail on,
Kingdom's keeper, counsel to follow,
Not to go to the guardian of the gold-
    hoard, but let him</td><td></td></tr>
<tr><td>25</td><td>Lie where he long was, live in his
    dwelling
Till the end of the world. Met we a
    destiny
Hard to endure: the hoard has been
    looked at,
Been gained very grimly; too
    grievous the fate that[130]
The prince of the people pricked to
    come thither.</td><td></td></tr>
<tr><td>30</td><td>*I* was therein and all of it looked at,
The building's equipments, since
    access was given me,
Not kindly at all entrance permitted
Within under earth-wall. Hastily
    seized I
And held in my hands a huge-
    weighing burden</td><td>He tells them of
Beowulf's last
moments.</td></tr>
<tr><td>35</td><td>Of hoard-treasures costly, hither out</td><td>Beowulf's dying</td></tr>
</table>

---

[128] For 'strude' in H.-So., S. suggests 'stride.' This would require 'ravage' (v. 16) to be changed to 'tread.'

[129] 'He cared ... sight of' (17, 18), S. emends so as to read as follows: *He (Beowulf) had not before seen the favor of the avaricious possessor.*

[130] B. renders: *That which drew the king thither* (i.e. *the treasure*) *was granted us, but in such a way that it overcomes us.*

<table>
<tr><td></td><td>bare them</td><td>request.</td></tr>
</table>

<pre>
     bare them   request.
     To my liegelord belovèd: life was yet
        in him,
     And consciousness also; the old one
        discoursed then
     Much and mournfully, commanded
        to greet you,
     Bade that remembering the deeds of
        your friend-lord
40   Ye build on the fire-hill of corpses a
        lofty
     Burial-barrow, broad and far-famous,
     As 'mid world-dwelling warriors he
        was widely most honored
     While he reveled in riches. Let us
        rouse us and hasten
     Again to see and seek for the
        treasure,
45   The wonder 'neath wall. The way I
        will show you,
     That close ye may look at ring-gems
        sufficient
     And gold in abundance. Let the bier
        with promptness
     Fully be fashioned, when forth we
        shall come,
     And lift we our lord, then, where
        long he shall tarry,
50   Well-beloved warrior, 'neath the   Wiglaf charges
        Wielder's protection."   them to build a
     Then the son of Wihstan bade orders   funeral-pyre.
        be given,
     Mood-valiant man, to many of
        heroes,
     Holders of homesteads, that they
        hither from far,
     [131]Leaders of liegemen, should look
        for the good one
55   With wood for his pyre: "The flame
        shall now swallow
</pre>

---

[131] 'Folc-ágende' (3114) B. takes as dat. sing. with 'gódum,' and refers it to Beowulf; that is, *Should bring fire-wood to the place where the good folk-ruler lay.*

(The wan fire shall wax[132]) the
    warriors' leader
Who the rain of the iron often abided,
When, sturdily hurled, the storm of
    the arrows
Leapt o'er linden-wall, the lance
    rendered service,
60 Furnished with feathers followed the
    arrow."
Now the wise-mooded son of
    Wihstan did summon
The best of the braves from the band
    of the ruler
Seven together; 'neath the enemy's
    roof he
Went with the seven; one of the
    heroes
65 Who fared at the front, a fire-blazing
    torch-light
Bare in his hand. No lot then decided
Who that hoard should havoc, when
    hero-earls saw it
Lying in the cavern uncared-for
    entirely,
Rusting to ruin: they rued then but
    little
70 That they hastily hence hauled out
    the treasure,
The dear-valued jewels; the dragon
    eke pushed they,
The worm o'er the wall, let the wave-
    currents take him,
The waters enwind the ward of the
    treasures.
There wounden gold on a wain was
    uploaded,
75 A mass unmeasured, the men-leader
    off then,
The hero hoary, to Whale's-Ness was
    carried.

He takes seven thanes, and enters the den.

They push the dragon over the wall. The hoard is laid on a wain.

---

[132] C. proposes to take 'weaxan' = L. 'vescor,' and translate *devour*. This
gives a parallel to 'fretan' above. The parenthesis would be discarded and
the passage read: *Now shall the fire consume, the wan-flame devour, the
prince of warriors, etc.*

XLIII.
The Burning of Beowulf

The folk of the Geatmen got him then ready
A pile on the earth strong for the burning,
Behung with helmets, hero-knights' targets,
And bright-shining burnies, as he begged
    they should have them;

5   Then wailing war-heroes their world-famous
      chieftain,
Their liegelord beloved, laid in the middle.
Soldiers began then to make on the barrow
The largest of dead-fires: dark o'er the vapor
The smoke-cloud ascended, the sad-roaring
    fire,

10   Mingled with weeping (the wind-roar
     subsided)
Till the building of bone it had broken to
    pieces,
Hot in the heart. Heavy in spirit
They mood-sad lamented the men-leader's
    ruin;
And mournful measures the much-grieving
    widow

15   *   *   *   *   *   *
      *   *   *   *   *   *
      *   *   *   *   *   *
      *   *   *   *   *   *
      *   *   *   *   *   *

20   *   *   *   *   *   *
The men of the Weders made accordingly
A hill on the height, high and extensive,
Of sea-going sailors to be seen from a
    distance,
And the brave one's beacon built where the
    fire was,

25   In ten-days' space, with a wall surrounded it,
As wisest of world-folk could most worthily
    plan it.
They placed in the barrow rings and jewels,
All such ornaments as erst in the treasure
War-mooded men had won in possession:

30   The earnings of earlmen to earth they
    entrusted,

Side-glosses:

Beowulf's pyre.

The funeral-flame.

The Weders carry out their lord's last request.

Rings and gems are laid in the barrow.

They mourn for

The gold to the dust, where yet it remaineth   their lord,
As useless to mortals as in foregoing eras.   and sing
'Round the dead-mound rode then the   his praises.
    doughty-in-battle,
Bairns of all twelve of the chiefs of the
    people,
35 More would they mourn, lament for their
    ruler,
Speak in measure, mention him with
    pleasure,
Weighed his worth, and his warlike
    achievements
Mightily commended, as 'tis meet one praise
    his
Liegelord in words and love him in spirit,
40 When forth from his body he fares to   An ideal
    destruction.   king.
So lamented mourning the men of the Geats,
Fond-loving vassals, the fall of their lord,
Said he was kindest of kings under heaven,
Gentlest of men, most winning of manner,
45 Friendliest to folk-troops and fondest of
    honor.

Addenda.

SEVERAL discrepancies and other oversights have been noticed in the H.-So. glossary. Of these a good part were avoided by Harrison and Sharp, the American editors of Beowulf, in their last edition, 1888. The rest will, I hope, be noticed in their fourth edition. As, however, this book may fall into the hands of some who have no copy of the American edition, it seems best to notice all the principal oversights of the German editors.

From hám (194).—Notes and glossary conflict; the latter not having been altered to suit the conclusions accepted in the former.

Þær gelýfan sceal dryhtnes dóme (440).—Under 'dóm' H. says 'the might of the Lord'; while under 'gelýfan' he says 'the judgment of the Lord.'

Eal bencþelu (486).—Under 'benc-þelu' H. says *nom. plu.*; while under 'eal' he says *nom. sing.*

Heatho-ræmas (519).—Under 'ætberan' H. translates 'to the Heathoremes'; while under 'Heatho-ræmas' he says 'Heathoræmas reaches Breca in the swimming-match with Beowulf.' Harrison and Sharp (3d edition, 1888) avoid the discrepancy.

Fáh féond-scaða (554).—Under 'féond-scaða' H. says 'a gleaming sea-monster'; under 'fáh' he says 'hostile.'

Onfeng hraðe inwit-þancum (749).—Under 'onfón' H. says 'he *received* the maliciously-disposed one'; under 'inwit-þanc' he says 'he *grasped*,' etc.

Níð-wundor séon (1366).—Under 'níð-wundor' H. calls this word itself *nom. sing.*; under 'séon' he translates it as accus. sing., understanding 'man' as subject of 'séon.' H. and S. (3d edition) make the correction.

Forgeaf hilde-bille (1521).—H., under the second word, calls it instr. dat.; while under 'forgifan' he makes it the dat. of indir. obj. H. and S. (3d edition) make the change.

Brád and **brún-ecg** (1547).—Under 'brád' H. says 'das breite Hüftmesser mit bronzener Klinge'; under 'brún-ecg' he says 'ihr breites Hüftmesser mit blitzender Klinge.'

Yðelíce (1557).—Under this word H. makes it modify 'ástód.' If this be right, the punctuation of the fifth edition is wrong. See H. and S., appendix.

Sélran gesóhte (1840).—Under 'sél' and 'gesécan' H. calls these two words accus. plu.; but this is clearly an error, as both are nom. plu., pred. nom. H. and S. correct under 'sél.'

Wið sylfne (1978).—Under 'wið' and 'gesittan' H. says 'wið = near, by'; under 'self' he says 'opposite.'

þéow (2225) is omitted from the glossary.

For duguðum (2502).—Under 'duguð' H. translates this phrase, 'in Tüchtigkeit'; under 'for,' by 'vor der edlen Kriegerschaar.'

þær (2574).—Under 'wealdan' H. translates *þær* by 'wo'; under 'mótan,' by 'da.' H. and S. suggest 'if' in both passages.

Wunde (2726).—Under 'wund' H. says 'dative,' and under 'wæl-bléate' he says 'accus.' It is without doubt accus., parallel with 'benne.'

Strengum gebæded (3118).—Under 'strengo' H. says 'Strengum' = mit Macht; under 'gebæded' he translates 'von den Sehnen.' H. and S. correct this discrepancy by rejecting the second reading.

Bronda be láfe (3162).—A recent emendation. The fourth edition had 'bronda betost.' In the fifth edition the editor neglects to change the glossary to suit the new emendation. See 'bewyrcan.'